Steve Parish

Amazing Facts about Australia's
Early Explorers

Photography: Steve Parish

Text: Karin Cox

Contents

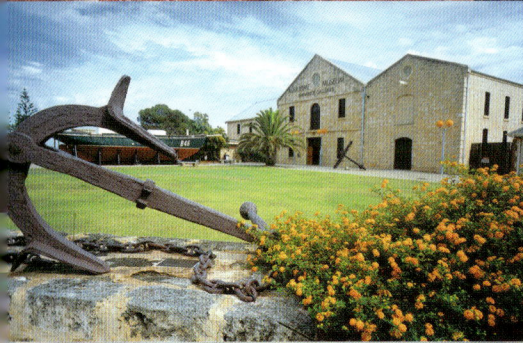

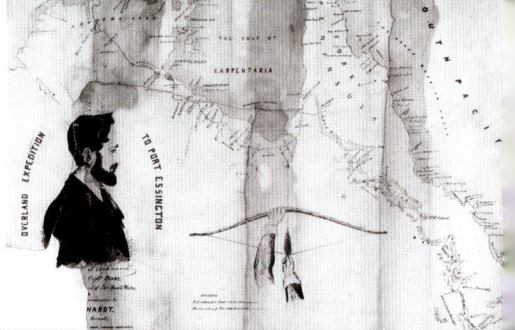

Above: A prau off Australia's northern coast.

the FACTS!

IN AROUND 140 AD, ancient Greek geographer Ptolemy wrote in his book *Geography* that the world was spherical. He believed in a landmass, which he called *Terra Incognita*, south of the Equator, which would "balance out" the continents in the north.

SOME PEOPLE REFUSED to believe in a Great Southern Land at all. One 6th century cosmographer, Cosmas Indicopleustes, believed that the Earth was oblong or box-shaped and laughed at the idea of southern continents, where he imagined people must have had to hang from the ceiling like flies or walk around upside down!

MACASSAN TRADERS and sea cucumber fishermen from the Celebes (now Sulawesi) were known to visit the coast of the Northern Territory from the early 1500s. These people probably first brought domesticated dogs to Australian shores, which later bred to become the Dingo (below).

TALL STORIES from the 1300s added to the mystery of exploration. In the 14th century, adventurers told imaginative tales of what they had seen. In *The Voyage and Travels of Sir John Mandeville, Knight*, the author describes a race of cannibalistic people with dog's heads living in India!

The search
for the Great Southern Land

As soon as philosophers began to believe that the world was round, speculation about an enormous southern landmass grew. The quest for gold, riches and spices urged seafaring empires to seek out this great "unknown" southern land.

BY THE 1400s, technological advances in ship-building, science and navigation ushered in an era of exploration and discovery in Europe and the East. Spain, Portugal, Holland, France and Britain — spurred on by the wealth the Italian Marco Polo described in the late 1200s — began to realise they too could exploit the resources of new lands, as well as spread their preferred religion and way of life to the countries they colonised, and become empires.

The Spanish and Portuguese were the first to broaden their horizons. When Portuguese explorer Batholomeu Diaz rounded the Cape of Good Hope in 1488, he discovered a sea route to the spice- and silk-rich countries to the east. His success was followed by that of his compatriot, Vasco da Gama, who reached India in 1497–98. With the support of Spain, Italian Christopher Columbus set off in 1492 to explore the east for himself, reaching islands he named the "West Indies" and going on to discover the "New World" — the Americas.

SUCH A RUSH OF TERRITORY up for grabs, coupled with an unstable relationship between Spain and Portugal, led Pope Alexander VI, under the 1494 Treaty of Tordesillas, to divide the world and all of its yet undiscovered lands into two halves. He decreed that any new countries to the east were to belong to Spain while those in the west would belong to Portugal. Obviously, by the time Australia was discovered, everyone ignored this decision! By 1770, when Briton James Cook claimed Australia's east coast for England as "New South Wales", England was at war with Spain and certainly ignored any decree made in 1494. The Dutch, who declared their independence from Spanish rule in 1581, also ignored the Pope's "rule" when Jansz discovered "New Holland" in 1606.

IN 1503 a Frenchman named Paulmier de Gonneville claimed to have been swept from the Cape of Good Hope onto a shore in the Southern Ocean, which he named *Terre Australe*. Gonneville claimed he stayed there for six months, before returning, with the son of a native king, to France. He relayed his account to the French navy but insisted that his journals were lost in a later pirate attack. The lack of accurate navigational records made it impossible for the authorities to verify that he had indeed found this "Gonneville Land" he spoke of.

Above: In 1494, the Treaty of Tordesillas split new discoveries between the naval "super powers" of Spain and Portugal.

New land or someone's backyard?

Who would be the first to find and map this vacant new land? Unbeknownst to the rest of the world, Aboriginal peoples had already inhabited this "unknown" continent for more than 50,000 years.

THE PORTUGUESE POSSIBILITY

There is some evidence that the Portuguese discovered and mapped part of Australia's east coast in the 1500s. In *The Secret Discovery of Australia,* Kenneth McIntyre claims that captain Christovao de Mendonca came ashore near Geelong sometime from 1522–24. He also suggests that a shipwreck known as the Mahogany Ship, discovered near Warrnambool in 1936, was one of Mendonca's ships. The Portuguese traded widely in the East Indies, so it may be that they were aware of the Great Southern Land but chose to keep the information to themselves.

UNFORTUNATELY, THE WRECK of the supposed Mahogany Ship was covered by sand and all attempts to find it again have failed, although a portion of the ship's wood, kept by local J. F. Archibald, was recently radiocarbon-dated to between 1660 and 1710 — well after the Dutch had visited this continent. By 1526, the Portuguese had found Timor and New Guinea and built ports in Malaya and Indonesia, which they called the Spice Islands. A 1542 map made in France (supposedly from Portuguese originals) shows that they probably did reach Australia.

CHINESE CAPERS

In 1879, a figurine carved from soapstone (left) was found stuck in the roots of a banyan tree near where Darwin stands today. It depicts the Chinese god of long life, Shou Lao, and was at first thought to date to the Ming dynasty, indicating that the Chinese may have visited Australia in the 1400s — long before Europeans. The figurine is now held at Sydney's Powerhouse Museum, where curators believe it is probably a 19th-century piece that arrived in Australia with Chinese migrants. However, from around 860 AD, Chinese merchants were known to trade in Africa and were aware of Indonesia, so it is possible that the Chinese were also early, yet unrecorded, visitors to these shores.

GEOGRAPHIC BLUNDERS

In 1574, a map created by Abraham Ortelius showed an enormous continent that covered almost the entire bottom half of the world. He had labelled it *Terra Australis Incognita* — the Unknown South Land. This supposed land was larger than both Australia and Antarctica combined.

IN THE 16TH CENTURY, England was occupied with internal battles of succession, wars with the French and religious matters; they had little interest in beating the Portuguese in the search for new continents. A map created in 1527 under the reign of King Henry VII even left a big blank space where Australia should be. The Dutch, however, were more convinced that a valuable land might be found at the southern extremity of the world. A 1594 Dutch map depicted an area called *Terra Australis*, but its shape and location were incorrect. From the 15th century, Arab and Middle Eastern seamen sailed the seas from Africa to China and possibly came into contact with the north coast of Australia.

What happened WHEN?

55 MILLION YEARS AGO The supercontinent Gondwana begins to break up. Australia moves away from Antarctica.

50,000 YEARS AGO+ Humans first appear in Australia.

18,000 BC Height of the Ice Age; Aborigines living in Tasmania.

13,000 BC Ice Age ends.

12,000 BC Sea covers land bridge to Tasmania.

140 AD Ptolemy, in *Geography,* writes that the world is spherical.

1000 AD Macassans begin to visit Australian waters.

1200 AD Aborigines in Victoria build stone huts.

1275 AD Venetian Marco Polo reaches China.

1405–33 AD Chinese junks may have reached Australia.

1488 AD Diaz rounds the Cape of Good Hope.

1492 AD Christopher Columbus crosses the Atlantic Ocean.

1497–98 AD Vasco da Gama reaches India.

1519–22 AD Ferdinand Magellan circumnavigates the world.

1522–24 AD Portuguese ships may have reached Australia.

1545 AD Yñigo Ortiz de Retez charts the New Guinea coast and calls it *Nova Guinea.*

Above: Australian Aborigines lived well off the land and many still do today.

the FACTS!

THE WORD ABORIGINAL means "from the beginning".

DNA RESEARCH conducted by geneticists at the University of Cambridge in the UK claims to have debunked the idea that Australian Aborigines developed in isolation, separate to human evolution in Africa. Evidence has been found of a genetic link between Aborigines and New Guineans, which indicates that both groups of people are descendants of humans who migrated from Africa between 55,000 and 60,000 years ago.

TASMANIAN Aboriginal groups knew how crucial fire was to survival, so they made it a point to share fire with both allies and enemies alike.

DREAMING SITES are believed to be places where ancestral spirits paused on their journey and created the landscape.

SOME ROCK ART (below) records the coming of foreigners and shows different customs.

UNTIL THE END OF THE LAST Ice Age, sea levels were 120–140 m lower than they are today.

The earliest
Australian adventurers

Little did the Europeans realise that a race of accomplished seafarers had already settled the Australian continent. There are no records of how Aborigines achieved this feat, but they most likely paddled from Asia in small, sturdy rafts and canoes.

FOR APPROXIMATELY 55,000 YEARS or more, Indigenous Australians have peopled this continent. In times of lower sea levels, a land bridge from Asia allowed passage to the Indonesian archipelago; from there, only a dangerous sea-going voyage in a well-built fishing craft — whether by chance or choice — separated humans from Australia.

These first discoverers of the southern continent must have been astonished by what they found — a vast land inhabited by strange animals and gigantic beasts known as megafauna. Despite the challenges they would have faced, the Australian Aborigines grew to understand the seasons, find food (both plant and animal), build weapons, tools and shelters, create kinship systems and forge a unique, spiritual culture.

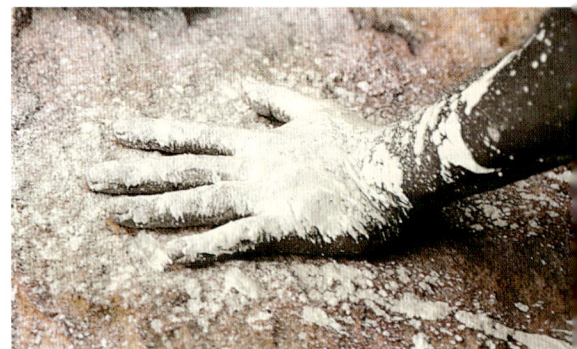

Above: Artwork of ochre on rock records spirits, people, places, events and myths.

Left: Body paint, music and dance are important elements of ceremonies.

BY THE TIME OF EUROPEAN OCCUPATION, there were numerous groups of Aboriginal people living all over the continent. Most cohabited in small family groups, or tribes, of 15–30 people. Each group shared a common language and law to ensure that social interactions were appropriate and sacred sites, rituals and ceremonies were properly observed. As they do today, elders passed knowledge from generation to generation by oral tradition, such as Creation (or Dreaming) stories, via dance and song during ceremonies or in artwork recorded on rock faces, paintings and carvings.

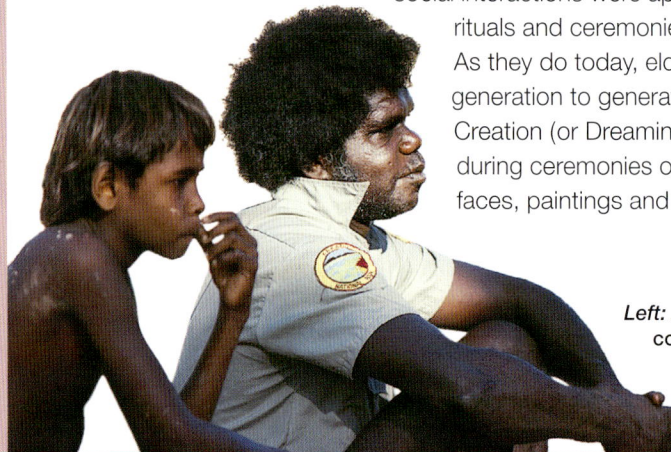

Left: Aborigines have a strong spiritual connection with this land and many work as guides in national parks to help preserve sites of traditional significance.

First Europeans to record
Australian shores

Above: A replica of the *Duyfken* built by the Western Australia Maritime Museum.

By 1600, Spain and Portugal had sailed much of the Pacific. Surely it was just a matter of time before they stumbled across the continent at the world's end? Surprisingly, however, the honour of discovery falls to a small Dutch ship.

ESTABLISHMENT of the wealthy Dutch East India Company in 1602 enabled the newly formed Dutch Republic, with its superior square-rigged trade ships, to steal trade from the Spanish and Portuguese in South-East Asia and the Pacific. With Dutch supremacy on the rise and tales of more riches in a land to the south, it was not long before Dutch authorities instructed navigator Willem Jansz "to discover the great land of Nova Guinea and other East and South lands".

IN COMMAND of the small, three-masted trading vessel the *Duyfken,* with a crew of just 20 men, Jansz set sail from Bantam, Indonesia, in 1605. The vessel was forced southwards from the coast of New Guinea by shoal water, reaching the Gulf of Carpentaria and making the first documented sighting of the Australian mainland — the coast of Cape York near the Pennefather River.

UNFORTUNATELY FOR JANSZ, he failed to realise that the coast he sailed along was not part of New Guinea. When Willem Jansz and a small group of men travelled upriver to make landfall, local Aborigines refused to let them land and speared and killed one of the men, bringing the number of deaths on board the *Duyfken* to nine — almost half the crew! Eight crewmen had earlier lost their lives to cannibals in New Guinea. With so many deaths, provisions of food and water running low and no sign of the fabled riches of the Great Southern Land, Jansz headed for home.

THE WEARY CREW of the *Duyfken* arrived back in Banda, an Indonesian island, in mid-1606 — just months shy of Portuguese sailor Torres finding the strait that lay to the north-east. Had they known of the strait's existence, Jansz may well have realised the importance of his discovery. As it was, the disappointing voyage curbed Dutch interest in that area of the coast until 1623.

the FACTS!

IN DUTCH, the word duyfken means "little dove".

JAN ROOSSENGIN, an official from the Dutch East India Company, actually shared command of the *Duyfken* with Willem Jansz, but little is known of him and he rarely rates a mention in the history books.

WILLEM JANSZ was given the nickname "I say, I say" because he used the phrase so much.

LATER IN HIS LIFE Jansz was honoured with the position of Admiral of the Dutch Fleet.

WHEN JANSZ and his men tried to go ashore south of where Weipa is today, one of his men was speared by Wik Aboriginal people and died. Jansz decided to go no further south, he turned the *Duyfken* around and named the place Cape Keerweer, which means "turn about" in Dutch.

THE WIK PEOPLE still occupy the territory near Cape Keerweer. Their stories tell of how they defeated the Dutchmen who tried to settle there.

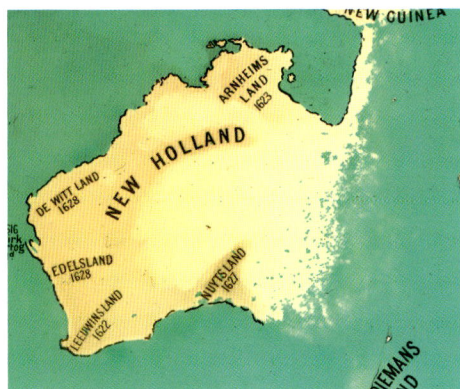

Above: For many years, Dutch cartographers reproduced Jansz's error, linking New Guinea to Cape York.

Above: The *Duyfken* in the Gulf of Carpentaria. Jansz charted about 300 km of Cape York Peninsula's west coast but failed to find the strait.

Above: Along with cargo and trade goods, the ship's hold was packed with provisions.

Above: Pedro de Quiros (1563–1615).

Pedro de Quiros
to Dirk Hartog

In 1605, the same year Jansz was given his orders to seek "the great land of Nova Guinea and other East and South lands" in the Duyfken, *Portuguese navigators Pedro de Quiros and Luis Vaez de Torres were sent on a three-ship Spanish-funded mission.*

SAILING WESTWARDS FROM PERU on the *St Paulo y St Pedro*, de Quiros reached Vanuatu in May 1606. He was enchanted by rumours of a southern wonderland and believed he had found outlying islands of the fabled continent. In tribute to Spain's Austrian allies, he named the land *Austrialia del Espiritu Santo,* which means South Land of the Holy Spirit.

Later in their journey, South East Trade Winds swept de Quiros' ship out to sea, leaving Torres (second-in-command aboard the ship *San Pedrico*, with the *Los Treyes* nearby) separated from his captain. Fifteen days later, realising de Quiros was unable to return, Torres set sail south-west before changing tack in the open ocean to sail north-west to New Guinea. In doing so, he passed through the strait that bears his name — the Torres Strait — proving that the land to the south was separate from New Guinea.

the FACTS!

DE QUIROS (above) returned to Spain and told imaginative tales about what he had seen. In a petition to King Philip III of Spain, requesting funds for more voyages, he wrote, *"The riches consisted of silver and pearls, which I saw myself, and gold which the other captain saw … There is likewise an abundance of nutmegs, mastic, pepper, ginger … Cinnamon is known there and cloves probably too"*.

TORRES' REPORT of his findings was kept secret for about 150 years because the Spanish were wary of the Portuguese or English exploring south of the strait.

HARTOG'S ORIGINAL PLAQUE was removed and replaced with a plaque by another Dutch explorer, Willem de Vlamingh, in 1697. It was then lost for many years until it was rediscovered in 1902. The plaque is now held in the Rijksmuseum in Amsterdam, the Netherlands.

EENDRACHT MEANS "concord", but is sometimes also translated as "unity" or "harmony".

DUTCH OFFICIALS called the area Hartog found "Eendrachtsland".

THE MALKANA Indigenous peoples inhabited the place where Hartog nailed up his plaque.

Above: An illustration from the *Picturesque Atlas of Australasia*, Volume I, 1886, shows Torres' ships. Torres is believed to have come within 200 km of the north-east coast — but whether he actually sighted this part of Australia or not remains unknown.

Above: Dirk Hartog Island, off the Western Australian coast.

MAKING AN IMPRESSION

The Dutch routinely travelled from Holland to the East Indies around the Cape of Good Hope, but in 1611 Captain Hendrik Brouwer found a better way — using the strong Roaring Forties winds he cut down his sailing time by many months. On this route, just a slight miscalculation could blow a ship further east — onto the Western Australian coast. This is precisely what happened to Dirk Hartog, captain of the *Eendracht* in October 1616. Hartog landed on the island now named after him and recorded his visit on a pewter plate.

Near-miss
navigators

Above and top right: Today the isolated Houtman Abrolhos Islands are home to lobster fishers.

Many Dutch ships accidentally ended up on Australia's west coast from 1616 to 1630, but the Dutch were so absorbed with trade that they maintained little interest in what lay south of the East Indies until much later on.

CAPTAINS WHO ended up sailing to Australia mostly recorded their mistake, but gave scant information about the land they sighted. Many accounts simply express dismay at the barren landscape. On 11 May 1618, in his ship the *Zeewolf*, Haevick Claeszoon landed north-west of where Onslow stands today. He was followed by Captain Leenaert Jacobsz, piloting the *Mauritius*, in the same year. One of the more positive accounts is that of Frederick de Houtman, who in 1619 landed just south of where Perth now stands, deeming it "a fine country". In honour of the councillor of the East Indies, Jacob Dedel, he named the area Dedelsland. Later, he just escaped wrecking his ship, the *Dordrecht*, on the coral shoals of the Houtman Abrolhos Islands.

Above: The *Tryal* was the first English ship to sight Australia, but was shipwrecked on the voyage.

Above: Arnhem Land was named by Dutch navigator Willem van Colster.

AN ENGLISH TRADING SHIP called the *Tryal,* which was bound for Siam with a load of silver, was less lucky than the *Dordrecht*. It struck the coast in 1622 and 97 people perished. The same year, the *Leeuwin* sighted the headland on the south-western corner of the continent, which now bears the name Cape Leeuwin. Another Dutch ship, the *Wapen van Hoorn*, ran aground near Shark Bay.

FINALLY, IN 1623 the Dutch decided to investigate further. Sailing the *Pera* and the *Arnhem* respectively, Jan Carstensz and Willem van Colster were despatched to explore the area Jansz found 17 years earlier. Carstensz found it "the driest, poorest area to be found in the world". Later, van Colster, in the *Arnhem*, was blown across the Gulf of Carpentaria to "islands and vast lands"— Arnhem Land.

Left: Cape Leeuwin Lighthouse on the rugged south coast of Western Australia.

the FACTS!

ABROLHOS is a Portuguese word meaning "look out" — so many navigators ran aground on the Houtman Abrolhos Islands that it is a very apt name.

JOHN BROOKE, the captain of the wrecked *Tryal*, and his first mate Thomas Bright sailed two longboats carrying 46 survivors from the shipwreck to Batavia. The governor-general later reported that the fate of another 97 persons was "known to God alone".

KLAAS HERMANSZOON landed the *Leiden* south of Dirk Hartog Island in 1623. While they were there, a baby was born, making this spot the birthplace of Australia's first European-descended child.

CAPTAIN DANIEL COCK later sailed the *Leiden* from the Zuytdorp Cliffs to Dirk Hartog Island in 1626, but did not make any landings.

IN 1627, Peter Nuyts and commander Francois Thijssen sailed the *Gulden Zeepaard* (Dutch for "golden seahorse") from the south coast of Western Australia about 1500 km to the Nuyts Archipelago, near Ceduna in South Australia.

NUYTS, who was the governor of Formosa (Taiwan), was kidnapped by Japanese traders in 1629. Luckily, he was freed within a week.

ALTHOUGH CARSTENSZ was unimpressed with the land he found, on the morning of 8 May 1623 his journal entry indicates that he went ashore and "gathered excellent vegetables or pot-herbs". What they were is not recorded.

CARSTENSZ LEFT an engraved wooden board on Cape York Peninsula marking his discovery and naming of the Staaten River.

Above: Sailing a tall ship certainly wasn't easy.

Life on the
open seas

Until navigators realised that the strong winds of the Roaring Forties could speed up their journey, it took a year or more to sail from Europe to the East Indies or New Holland. For the captain and crew, the voyage was long and arduous.

Limited navigational technology made staying on course a constant problem.

BEFORE the 19th century, captains sailed their ships using landmarks and celestial navigation — finding their way by the sun, stars and moon — along with handwritten accounts of routes and harbours (called rutters). Fog, smoke or clouds could obscure the sun and stars and even a small miscalculation could blow ships hundreds of kilometres off course!

Above: Sir Thomas Mitchell's sextant, used to measure the angle between the horizon and the sun.

the FACTS!

IN THE YEAR 1000, lodestone (magnetic iron ore) was discovered and it was found that it could make a needle point to the north. Early navigators began to float magnetised needles in bowls of water — the first compasses — to discover the direction north.

THE COMPASS was invented by the 1200s and from the 1400s European countries sent people to explore in earnest.

THE BRITISH GOVERNMENT offered a £20,000 reward to anyone who could solve the problem of longitude. John Harrison got the reward in 1762 by inventing the seagoing chronometer — a clock that kept precise time at sea, making calculating longitude more accurate.

IT WASN'T UNTIL 1767 that the first Nautical Almanac was published by British Astronomer Royal Neville Maskelyne. It recorded lunar distances to help navigators figure out longitude.

IN 1884, the majority of nations agreed to make the Prime Meridian line run through Greenwich, England. In the same way that the Equator divides the Earth into Northern and Southern Hemispheres, the Prime Meridan divides the world into eastern and western halves; all places on Earth are measured from their distance east or west of this line.

Above: More of James Cook's navigational instruments, which include star symbols, dates, compass, sundial and spirit level.

FROM THE 1400s, sailors were constantly seeking better methods of navigation. The main instruments used were the compass, quadrant, and astrolabe or cross-staff — a simpler version of the astrolabe that gave the same information. Improvements on the design of the cross-staff led to the invention of the quadrant, which developed into navigational devices, such as the sextant and octant, that are used today. These tools were less useful in the Southern Hemisphere until the 1600s, when astronomers began to include maps of the southern constellations in their star charts.

NAVIGATIONAL TOOLS were useful for charting latitude, but navigators also had to figure out the ship's longitude, which was much harder. Navigators used rough calculations of speed and directions, known as "dead reckoning", to help them discern latitude. Dead reckoning was all right over short distances, but on long ocean-going journeys even a tiny error could lead to disaster! Later, the invention of the seagoing chronometer made calculating longitude much easier.

AYE, AYE CAPTAIN!

A very important part of a sailor's training to become a captain was that he must be able to navigate and keep accurate written records of each journey. In return for this responsibility, the captain usually enjoyed better provisions than the crew.

SENSIBLE CAPTAINS generally kept a log of the crew and passengers on board the vessel, listing their names and their roles. By the 18th century, this was essential for British ships because an Act of Parliament passed in 1747 decreed that muster rolls must be kept, detailing who sailed on every ship.

THOSE LUCKY ENOUGH to sit at the captain's table would have occasionally feasted on chicken or pork if there were animals on board. It was also the captain's duty to ensure that the crew had enough food and did not suffer from malnutrition.

When supervising the crew, captains had to be firm but fair. If they were too strict, the crew might become mutinous and throw the ship into chaos.

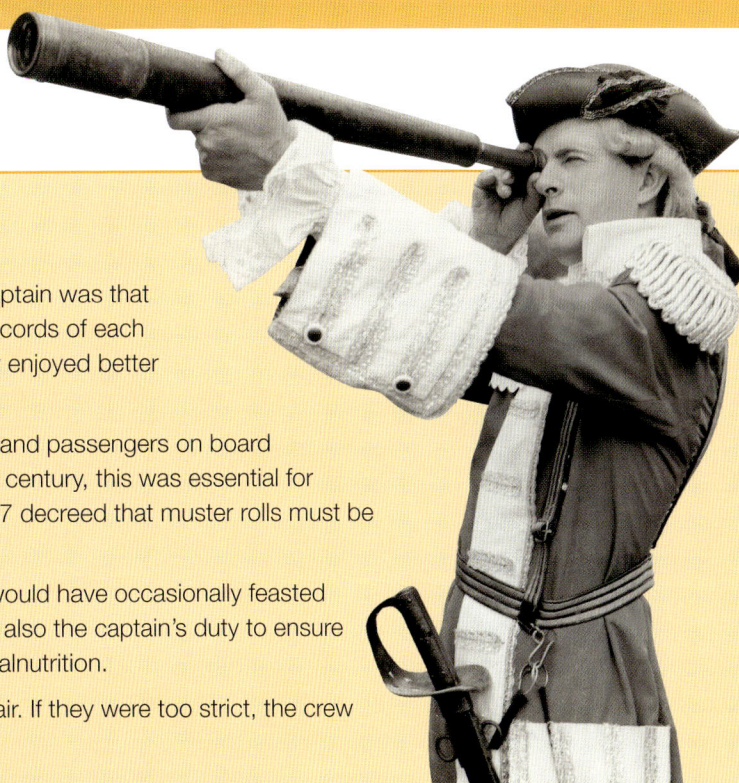

CRAMPED QUARTERS

Most ships were very crowded. Usually, the captain had his own cabin while most of the crew slept on deck or in hammocks in the hold. Wealthy passengers or scientific staff often shared the captain's cabin. On the *Endeavour,* Captain Cook did not have a cabin to himself — instead, he shared the "Great Cabin" with Banks and the other men of standing on board the vessel. Men who slept in the hold shared their "bedroom" with provisions, clothes, spare sails, ropes and other essential items for a sea journey of twelve months or more.

Above: A view below deck on the replica *Dufyken* built at the Fremantle Maritime Museum.

Above: A cross-section of the *Endeavour,* showing the deck, cargo hold and cabins. The officers' cabins are on the lower deck, near the stern. Cabins were also fitted to the aft fall deck to make room for the many scientists and gentlemen on board.

NAVAL TERMINOLOGY

HOLD The bottom deck, where cargo and provisions are stored.

FATHOM A way of measuring depth. One fathom was about 1.8 m. To measure depth, sailors lowered a rope with a weight tied to it down to the seabed and took note of how much of the rope was lowered.

KNOT A way of measuring speed that equates to about 1.85 km/h. To measure the rate of knots they were travelling at, sailors dragged a length of rope, which was knotted at specific intervals, behind the boat. The number of knots that went overboard every 30 seconds was the rate of knots travelled.

LATITUDE A north–south distance calculation made by measuring the height of the sun (or stars) on the horizon.

LONGITUDE An east–west distance calculation that requires knowledge of the exact time at a particular location. Made easier by the invention of the seagoing chronometer.

Tough times
& hard tack

The crew suffered an uncomfortable time on a long sea voyage. Food was unappetising, privacy non-existent, and cleaning the ship was a boring and regular duty. For some, however, the delights of discovery far outweighed the discomforts of ship life!

Each member of the crew had a designated position and would have taken turns to go on watch, scrub the deck, hoist the sails, be responsible for cannons and other such tasks.

THERE WERE MANY RISKS involved with trading goods by sea or exploring far-flung lands around the globe. Storms, reefs and rough seas could destroy ships, or pirates might ambush a ship to plunder goods and cause mayhem. During wartime, enemy nations also often used to attack and rob each other's ships. Many a wealthy buccaneer (sometimes more politely called a privateer) made his fortune robbing other vessels. Buccaneers were not considered pirates. Their governments had usually given them written permission to plunder, providing that they handed over a share of the spoils when they returned home.

SHIPWRECK, MUTINY AND DISASTER

The Western Australian coastline proved treacherous for many ships. Among them was the *Batavia*, which ran aground on reefs near the Houtman Abrolhos Islands on 4 June 1629. Amazingly, the ship's commander, Francisco Pelsaert, and 47 others managed to cover 3000 km of open ocean in lifeboats to reach Batavia (now Jakarta) and send a rescue party. In the meantime, survivors on the scattered islands were terrorised by undermerchant Jeronimus Cornelisz and his bloodthirsty gang of mutineers, who hoped to steal the wreck's cargo, take over the rescue ship and engage in a life of piracy.

WHEN PELSAERT RETURNED it was to find that 125 men, women and children had been brutally butchered on the island that came to be known as "Batavia's Graveyard". With the help of soldier Wiebbe Hayes, nine mutineers were detained and executed, with the others taken to Batavia for punishment.

YEARS LATER, in 1712, another Dutch East India Company ship, the *Zuytdorp*, which had lost 112 of its 286 crew members to scurvy earlier in the journey, was wrecked near the dramatic cliffs that now bear the ship's name.

Above: An artist's impression of the violent scenes on "Batavia's Graveyard".

Above: The rugged Zuytdorp Cliffs, where the ship *Zuytdorp* came to ruin.

the FACTS!

BUCCANEER is a South American word. It means "dried meat" — a food which made up a large part of the sailors' diets.

MOST VESSELS carried cannons and artillery to ward off attack by pirates or unfriendly natives. The cannon below is mounted on the replica *Duyfken*, which, as a scouting ship, was armed.

FEW EUROPEAN SAILORS could swim, and when a ship sank many sailors drowned.

WARSHIPS and large trading ships were not the most suitable vessels for a long journey. To begin with they were expensive, but rough winds could also blow them onto reefs and destroy them.

TWO MUTINEERS from the *Batavia*, Wouter Loos and Jan Pelgrom de Bye, were marooned on the Western Australian mainland as punishment for their part in the atrocities. They can be said to be Australia's first white settlers. The men were never heard from again, but it is thought they may have been accepted into Aboriginal groups (based on some genetic differences in certain tribes). Any survivors of the *Zuytdorp* wreck might also have been befriended.

Tales of tragedy

The Shipwreck Gallery Maritime Museum in Fremantle (right) and Flagstaff Hill Maritime Museum in Warrnambool (far right) both contain artefacts from ships wrecked on Australia's coasts.

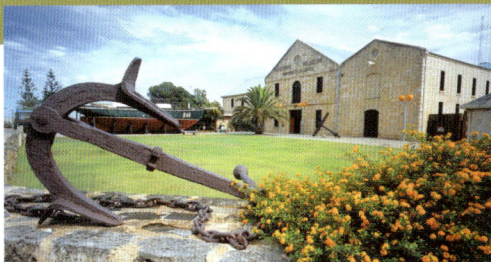

BORED ON BOARD

Life at sea could be tedious and dull. To keep boredom at bay, sailors might read, whittle or carve wood, play musical instruments, or sing and dance on deck. Food may have run low under Louis de Bougainville's command of the *Bordeuse*, but morale remained high and accounts report that the sailors remained cheerful and "danced on the deck each night". On board the *Endeavour*, one sailor kept himself occupied by carving intricate patterns on a coconut shell (left).

Coconut Carved By Sailor On The Endeavour

the FACTS!

ON BOARD the *Endeavour* were four pigs, a few dozen chickens, two greyhounds, three cats and a milking goat, as well as 18 months worth of supplies, and the crew.

THE GOAT THAT provided milk for the *Endeavour* had already circumnavigated the world! It had been on the frigate *Dolphin* under the command of Samuel Wallis.

LIMITED ingredients made meals very repetitive — on some ships, sailors could tell what day of the week it was by the food the cook dished up!

SUPPLIES ON BOUGAINVILLE'S ships, *La Boudeuse* and *L'Étoile*, ran extremely low — so low that sailors were forced to eat the ships' rats.

ON COOK'S *ENDEAVOUR* voyage, he made the crew drink lime juice and eat pickled cabbage to avoid contracting scurvy.

AFTER MANY MONTHS at sea, even the casks of water could become brackish. Sailors usually drank wine or beer and mixed their drinks with water to make the supplies last longer.

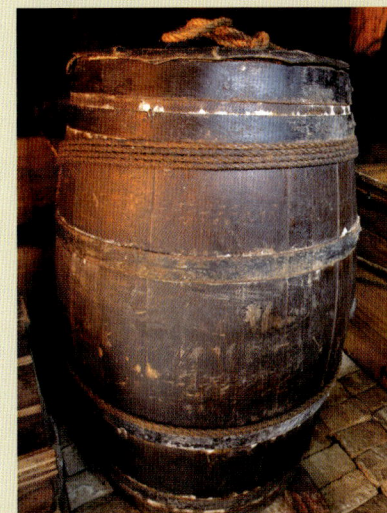

SURVIVING SCURVY

Although Europeans had begun to learn a lot about navigation, they still didn't know very much about medicine. Scurvy killed numerous men.

ON MANY SHIPS, especially well into the voyage, food was strictly rationed, often very bland and even "off" — or full of weevils. Fresh fruit and vegetables did not last long. Some fruits, such as citrus fruits, were especially hard to come by. The disease scurvy, caused by a lack of vitamin C, made the crew sick and claimed many lives on board. Whenever the ship reached shore, scouting parties had to be sent to search for fresh water and food that could be taken on board.

MEAT WAS ALSO SCARCE on board. Refrigeration was not yet possible, so meat was preserved by being dried and salted, with herbs and spices used to cover the smell of slightly rancid meat.

TO FILL THE SAILORS' hungry bellies, meals were usually supplemented by a type of tough, cracker-like biscuit known as "hard tack". This was made up of whole-wheat flour, salt and water. Only one hot meal a day was cooked on an oven made of a rough metal box that was open at the front and top and stacked with wood. Pans and griddles were placed on a grill over the fire or hung above the fire.

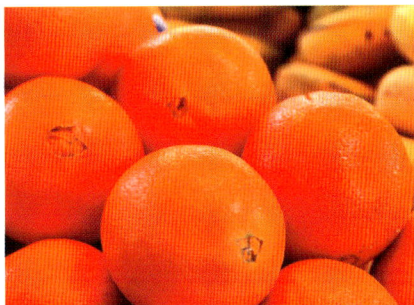

Above: Fresh fruit and vegetables provided the best defence against scurvy.

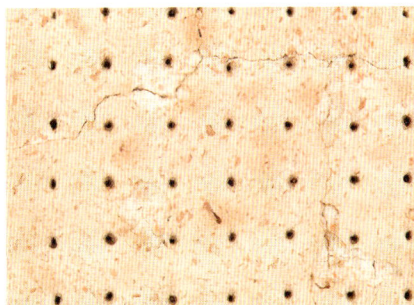

Above: During World War II, Arnott's made a hard tack biscuit for troops.

Above: Food was cooked on a rough oven made up of an open metal box filled with wood.

Above: Tribute to Dutch sailors in Tasmania.

the FACTS!

THE CREW of the *Turtelduyf* (or "turtledove" in English) encountered and named Turtelduyf Island in the Houtman Abrolhos group in 1624.

IN 1628, when Gerrit Frederikszoon de Witt's vessel, the *Vianen*, struck land between where Exmouth and Onslow are today, the crew was forced to throw 20 tonnes of valuable copper and pepper overboard to get the ship back afloat. De Witt recorded that he had landed on "the South Land Beyond Java". The Dutch called this area "De Witt's Land" for some time to come.

CAPTAIN WOOLEBRAND DE JONGH, of the yacht *Amsterdam*, sighted land near Shark Bay in 1635 but did not land.

VAN DIEMEN had been a crew member on the *Mauritius* in 1618, so he was excited about discovering more land for Holland.

GERRITT POOL and his steward, Andries Schiller, were hacked to death by natives (possibly cannibals) in New Guinea. Reports ominously suggest that pieces of their bodies were carried off, although, "*it never could be discovered what they did with them*".

BY 1644, the Dutch were keen to chart the outline of the Australian continent. A map labelled "Hollandia Novia", created by Justus Danckert, shows Australia's northern, western and southern coasts beginning to take shape.

IN 1648, the *Leeuwerik*, captained by Jan Janszoon Zeeuw, also charted some more of Australia's west coast, but again did not land.

Coen to Caen
— more Dutch sailors

When the ships Galias, Utrecht *and* Textel — *the convoy carrying Dutch East Indies Governor-General Jan Coen — struck a reef near the Houtman Abrolhos Islands in 1628, calls were made for better charts of this area of the coast to be produced.*

Above: Anthony van Diemen (1593–1645), governor-general of Batavia in 1632.

TOWARDS THE END OF 1628, the Dutch East India Company's official cartographer, Hessel Gerritz, had mapped a recognisable outline of the Western Australian coast. His map included the area recorded by de Witt and stretched south to Nuyt's Archipelago and the St Peter and St Francis Islands in the Great Australian Bight. Even with the magnitude of the coastline beginning to emerge, it was not until Anthony van Diemen succeeded Coen in the role of governor-general that the Dutch truly seized the opportunities to add to their territory in the Pacific.

VAN DIEMEN wasted little time once he came to office. In 1636 he immediately sent Gerrit Pool and Pieter Pietersz, in the *Klein Amsterdam* and *Wessel,* to further survey the coastline touched upon by Carstensz and Colster the decade before. It was also hoped they would find a route through the Torres Strait, seek out the whereabouts of the two men marooned on the mainland after the *Batavia* incident, and find a suitable place for the Dutch East India Company ships to stock up on fresh water and food between the latitudes of 26° and 28° south.

THE VOYAGE WAS NOT SUCCESSFUL. Pool was killed in New Guinea and Pietersz made it just south of the Cobourg Peninsula, which he named Van Diemen Gulf, sighting Melville Island and the Dundas Strait, before returning to Java.

AVIAN ODDITIES

The *Banda*, also under sail in 1636 and under the command of Antonie Caen, sighted the south-west coast just off Bernier Island. Here, possibly the first description of a Black Swan (right) was made.

Sixty-one years later, in 1697, Willem de Vlamingh was to be similarly astounded by these birds, which were believed to be zoologically impossible at the time. De Vlamingh captured two Black Swans and took them back to Batavia with him.

Trials & travels
— Abel Tasman

Undaunted by earlier missions, van Diemen put his faith in 39-year-old Captain Abel Jansz Tasman. In the Heemskerck *and* Zeehaen, *Tasman discovered Van Diemen's Land (Tasmania) before being blown east to New Zealand.*

TASMAN'S VOYAGE, while it did not accomplish what it set out to do (which was to ascertain whether the land to the south was joined to Antarctica or was an island, and to find "uncommonly large profit"), was nevertheless successful in part.

Above: The rocky spur of Tasman Island is named after this Dutch adventurer.

ON 3 DECEMBER 1642, Tasman claimed Van Diemen's Land for the Dutch. Strangely, he did not attempt to circumnavigate the island he had found; nor did he travel around New Zealand later in the journey. Tasman was impressed with Van Diemen's Land, writing:

> *Whoever perfectly discovers and settles it will become infallibly possessed of Territories as Rich, as fruitful, & as capable of Improvement, as any that have been hitherto found out, either in the East Indies or the West.*

TASMAN WORKED FOR the powerful Dutch East India Company, which made a fortune out of trading spices and wood from the East Indies (now Indonesia), and other luxury items such as silk, coffee, porcelain, gold and copper from around the world. In spite of Tasman's enthusiastic report, the company was disappointed. In 1644, van Diemen sent him on a second mission to figure out whether New Guinea, New Holland, Van Diemen's Land and the new land (New Zealand) were linked. On this voyage, Tasman charted much of the north Australian coast and all of the Gulf of Carpentaria before returning to Batavia.

the FACTS!

TASMAN'S JOURNEY was made for the dual purposes of discovery and trade. If Tasman found inhabitants, van Diemen instructed him to, "*parley with its rulers and subjects, letting them know you have landed there for the sake of commerce*".

THE STRANGE LIST of provisions on Tasman's vessels included 19 pounds of elephant teeth, 200 small Chinese wooden combs, a large brass basin and 2 packets of tinsel!

Above: Abel Tasman, depicted with his wife and daughter in 1637, in a painting believed to be by Jacob Gerritsz Cuyp.

TASMAN AND HIS CREW heard noises when they went ashore, but did not see any Aborigines. They did see footholds carved into a tree — the height of the footholds made them think the natives in that area must have been giants.

LATER IN HIS CAREER, Tasman became a buccaneer and tried to make his living from plundering Spanish ships.

Left: Abel Tasman's ships were the *Heemskerck* (Dutch for "home church"), which carried 60 men, and the *Zeehaen* ("sea cock" or "rooster"), which had a crew of 50.

Above: An oil painting of William Dampier (1651–1715) by William Dobson.

A daring buccaneer
— William Dampier

Englishman William Dampier may not have been the most orthodox navigator, but he was one of the most interesting. Exciting accounts of his travels, along with his detailed drawings of Australian plants and animals, earned him worldwide acclaim.

Dampier was born in East Coker, near Somerset, England, and joined the navy before becoming a privateer. In 1685, he joined the crew of the *Cygnet* under the command of Captain Charles Swan — a legitimate privateer turned pirate thanks to his out-of-control crew who were intent on plundering Spanish vessels.

WITH ANGRY SPANIARDS in pursuit, the *Cygnet's* best chance of escape was west into the Pacific. The trip usually took an average of 60 days, but food was scarce, so Dampier navigated the ship to Guam in just 51 days — luckily for him, because he later found that the crew had intended to eat Captain Swan and himself if they ran out of food!

Above: An engraved plate (London *c.* 1777) shows Dampier and his crew stealing oxen and mules laden with provisions.

The sailors later became mutinous again and abandoned Captain Swan in the Philippines, forcing Dampier to stay on board under the command of John Read. When the ship was washed ashore on the west coast of Australia in 1688, Dampier and the crew spent two months camping near King Sound, in the traditional country of the Bardi people, before setting sail for Cocos Island.

Below: Mudflats near King Sound on the Western Australian coast, where the *Cygnet's* crew stayed for two months.

the FACTS!

WHEN PLUMP CAPTAIN SWAN heard of the crew's plan to eat Dampier and himself if they ran out of food, he remarked to the lean Dampier, "Ah! Dampier, you would have made but a poor meal".

Above: An artist's rendition of Dampier's escape from the Nicobar Islands.

WHEN THE *CYGNET* reached the Nicobar Islands, Dampier and seven other men fled the villainous pirate crew and, amazingly, sailed a flimsy canoe (above) through wild seas to Sumatra. Once there, Dampier joined another ship and continued to make voyages trading goods. He only returned to England in September 1691.

WILLIAM DAMPIER believed that the Great Southern Land definitely existed. He claimed that a buccaneer acquaintance named Captain Davis had sighted this lucrative land at latitude 27° south.

A floral tribute

Dampier made many notes about the plants, animals and people he encountered, also illustrating them. The plant genus Dampiera is named after him.

BY THE TIME DAMPIER arrived back in England, he was a poor and penniless ex-privateer, but within six years his travelogue *A New Journey Around the World* would make him not only rich, but famous. He took up a position with British Customs; however, the thrills of discovery still beckoned. Dampier urged the Admiralty to fit out a ship that could be used to further explore the coast of New Holland. They decided that Dampier would be just the man for the job.

RETURNING IN THE *ROEBUCK*

Now a legitimate and respected navigator, Dampier was given the command of the *Roebuck*, a British warship, and in 1698 received instructions to sail in search of new lands via the Cape of Good Hope. He was to:

Survey all islands, shores, capes, bays, creeks and harbours fit for shelters as well as defence, to take careful soundings as he went, to note tides, currents, winds, and the character of the weather … to observe the disposition and commodities of the natives.

By this time, with years of experience under his belt, Dampier was a canny seaman and a trusted navigator. He took on board with him 50 crew members and provisions to feed them for 20 months, as well as twelve guns. In January 1699, the *Roebuck* set sail.

CAPTAIN DAMPIER STRUCK TROUBLE before they reached the first port. His second-in-command, Lieutenant Fisher, was insubordinate, so Dampier threw him off the ship when they reached Bahia in Brazil. Fisher was imprisoned there without a way of getting home — a fact that was to cause Dampier an unexpected headache when he returned to England. In 1702, Fisher had him court-martialled in England and Dampier was ruled not "a fit person to be employed as commander of any of Her Majesty's ships". Despite this falling out with the Admiralty, Dampier went on to command the privateer *St George* less than a year later and many more ships after that. However, back in 1699, with the wind of discovery in his sails, Dampier had no way of knowing what his decision to sack Fisher would bring, and set off south in the hope of discovering great wealth.

Above: Roebuck Bay, named after the vessel on Dampier's second voyage.

Above: The *Roebuck*, weighing 290 tonnes, was old and sprung a leak midway into the journey, forcing Dampier to sail for Timor.

UNRELIABLE *ROEBUCK*

Dampier sailed east from the Cape of Good Hope to the west coast of Australia, and named Shark Bay, before heading north as far as Roebuck Bay. On the way, he made many worthy observations; however, frustrated by the lack of available water and the limitations of the *Roebuck* (which was beginning to leak badly), he sailed to Timor for provisions and then on to New Guinea. The *Roebuck* was rotten and fast deteriorating by the time they reached Ascension Island in the Atlantic, where the crew abandoned the ship and had to be rescued by a passing ship to return to England.

FAME & FORTUNE

On his return to England, Dampier became very famous. His books, *A New Voyage Round the World*, *A Supplement to the Voyage Round the World*, *Two Voyages to Campeachy*, *A Discourse of Trade Winds* and the two-part *Voyage to New Holland*, were widely read and brought Dampier much acclaim.

SO WELL KNOWN were Dampier's exploits that author Johnathon Swift made out that his fictitious character, Lemuel Gulliver, in *Gulliver's Travels*, was Dampier's cousin.

ANOTHER FAMOUS BOOK also has a link to Dampier — *Robinson Crusoe*. In 1709 Dampier captained the ship that rescued Scotsman Alexander Selkirk from the Juan Fernandez Islands, off the coast of Chile. Selkirk was the real Robinson Crusoe, who went on to provide the inspiration for Daniel Defoe's famous tale of shipwreck.

Above: Charles de Brosses (1709–77).

IN 1697, WILLEM de Vlamingh set off in the *Geelvinck*, *Nijptangh* and *Weseltje* in search of a missing Dutch ship, the *Ridderschap van Holland*. On this journey, he explored from Swan River to North West Cape, landing at Cottesloe (where a memorial to him stands) and exploring Rottnest Island. He also discovered Dirk Hartog's pewter plate and replaced it with one of his own, which bears details of both expeditions. Cape Vlamingh (below) is named in his honour.

THE COAST OF ARNHEM LAND was explored in 1704 by Dutchman Maarten van Delft, who was sent to see whether it was likely the English would explore further.

CAPTAIN JAN STEYNS wrecked the *Zeewijk* in the Houtman Abrolhos Islands in 1727. Survivors built the first boat to be constructed by Europeans in Australia and sailed the makeshift *Sloepie* to Batavia.

THE LAST DUTCH exploration was in 1756 by Gonzal and van Asschen in the *Rijder* and *Buijs*.

FROM 1756 TO 1763, the Seven Years War between the British and the French left neither country much time for exploration.

More European
explorations

Following Dampier's account of his travels there was a 50-year pause in British interest in Australia. However, European traders remained eager for spoils. In time, authors and adventurers began to speculate that perhaps this land had more to offer after all …

In 1744, a man named John Campbell wrote a book suggesting that, despite Dampier's criticism of New Holland, there must be other fine regions or lands somewhere within such a large landmass.

CAMPBELL'S IDEA that the British should investigate further went unheeded, but twelve years later French author Charles de Brosses — spurred on by the start of the Seven Years War with Britain — suggested France might also benefit from forays into the Pacific. He wrote that New Holland might prove more worthy than Dampier had described. Perhaps, he suggested, France could start a new colony there by sending "criminals, vagabonds, beggars and orphans" to "reform" them into useful citizens. "The time to start these colonies is now, before the British get there," Brosses wrote. Little did he know that, when the British did "get there", this idea of a criminal colony would be adopted.

Above: Willem de Vlamingh explored and named Rottnest Island in 1697.

A HUGE, RICH LAND

By 1767, Torres' discovery of a strait to the south of New Guinea had come to light. Seizing on this and other evidence from the many Dutch ships that had recorded the coastline, Alexander Dalrymple, a well-known hydrographer and naturalist, published a book suggesting that the proposed "Great South Land" must exist. Because so many explorers had seen part of it, he was sure this was a "a huge land, a rich land". He also wrote that "it must be found and ruled by Britain".

Above: Alexander Dalrymple (1737–1808) was convinced of a "Great South Land" and urged Britain to seek its discovery.

The coming
of Cook

Above: Captain James Cook (1728–79).

By the 18th century, ongoing animosity between France and England, coupled with the loss of French territory in India and Canada, led to a race between the French and the British to claim new lands in the Southern Hemisphere.

The man who would be credited with claiming Australia as a British colony was Lieutenant (later Captain) James Cook, a 40-year-old ex-merchant seaman and Royal Navy man from Yorkshire. However, he was not the first Englishman sent to seek out the continent.

BEFORE HIM, Commodore John Byron had taken a hasty trip through the Pacific in the *Dolphin*. His lacklustre effort was followed by Samuel Wallis, who went on to discover Tahiti in the same vessel — inadvertently altering the course of history. Tahiti became the Admiralty's chosen location to send observers for the transit of Venus — a rare celestial event that would provide data for more accurate navigation in the Southern Hemisphere.

MEANWHILE, AWARE OF English intentions to find "Land or Islands of Great Extent … between Cape Horn and New Zealand" (as were Wallis' orders), Louis Antoine de Bougainville embarked on France's first expedition to the Pacific, commissioned in 1766. His aim was to circumnavigate the globe in the frigate *La Boudeuse* and the store ship *L'Étoile*. Secretly, the hoped-for result was for him to claim the Great Southern Land for France.

UNLUCKILY, Bougainville hit breakers just off the Great Barrier Reef. He had seen the much sought after east coast, but turned around, passing up the chance to make the continent a French colony. Cook's *Endeavour* sailed out of Plymouth on 25 August 1768 — the rest, as they say, is history!

Above: The British Admiralty purchased for Cook's voyage a small, flat-bottomed Whitby-built ship called the *Earl of Pembroke*, shown leaving Whitby Harbour in 1768. This 29.8 m converted coal carrier, renamed the HM Bark *Endeavour*, was to carry 94 men over thousands of kilometres of ocean.

Right: Cook's parents' cottage, in Fitzroy Gardens, Melbourne, was relocated piece by piece from Yorkshire in 1934.

the FACTS!

FRENCH NAVIGATOR de Surville could have thwarted Cook's discovery had it not been for a miscalculation made near the Santa Cruz Islands. This took him into the open ocean between Australia and New Zealand. Had he held this course he most likely would have ended up somewhere near Cook's landing, but he altered course and reached Doubtless Bay in New Zealand instead.

UNBEKNOWNST to Bougainville (below), his expedition carried a secret cargo — the first woman to circumnavigate the globe! When the ship reached Tahiti, the chief naturalist Philibert Commerçon's assistant was found to be a woman named Jeanne Baret, who had fooled them all by dressing as a man. Bougainville later wrote that once her true sex was revealed, "it was difficult to prevent the sailors from alarming her modesty".

ORIGINALLY, the Royal Society nominated Alexander Dalrymple to lead the *Endeavour* expedition to Tahiti to observe the transit of Venus. However, the Admiralty would not agree to put a non-navy person in charge of a ship, so Cook was appointed instead.

Above: Cook with his navigational maps.

Cook's life
& voyage of discovery

Captain Cook cannot truly be said to have discovered Australia, but over his lifetime he did venture into every one of the world's oceans, made a great many maps and named many places — possibly more than any other explorer.

the FACTS!

THE SHIP renamed the *Endeavour* was once a coal boat purchased for £2200 from a man named Thomas Milner. The ship was three years and nine months old when it began to be kitted out for the journey.

COOK WAS PAID 100 guineas by the Royal Society to observe the transit of Venus from Tahiti. The gold coin one guinea was worth 21 shillings. At the time, this could also buy a fine beaver hat; 12 French lessons, or pay for a tradesman's services for more than a week.

COOK, Green and Solander all observed the planetary event of Venus' transit across the sun and all made records, but the method they used was incorrect, so their observations were scientifically useless.

COOK NEITHER SPIED land first, nor made the first European footstep on Australia's east coast. Land was first sighted on 18 April 1770 by Lieutenant Zachary Hicks. Point Hicks is named after him.

NORTH OF Hervey Bay, someone on board cut off part of the clerk Richard Orton's ears while he lay in a drunken slumber! It was probably retaliation for telling tales to Cook about other men on board.

THE *ENDEAVOUR* even travelled into space! A part of the ship's stern was taken aboard the American spaceship *Endeavour I* in 1968.

Cook's orders were to sail to the newly discovered land of Tahiti to observe the passage of the planet Venus across the sun. At the time, navigation in the Southern Hemisphere was made difficult because few star charts showed constellations and planet positions in the southern sky. Viewing and measuring the Venus transit would make further exploration easier.

ON BOARD WERE men of great scientific standing — the Royal Observatory's astronomer Charles Green; a Swedish naturalist, Daniel Solander; and wealthy botanist Joseph Banks, who had part-funded the voyage. The ship also carried £10,000 worth of telescopes and other instruments from the Royal Society. A friend of Banks said they carried:

… all sorts of machines for catching and preserving insects, all types of nets, trawls, drags and hooks for coral fishing, they even have a curious contrivance of a telescope by which, put into the water, you can see the bottom at great depth.

Above: A replica of Cook's *Endeavour*, the *Young Endeavour* sailing at sunset.

COOK'S SECRET MISSION

Such an illustrious crew seemed to demand a more important mission than simply observing the stars, and a second part to the mission was later revealed. In Cook's cabin were secret orders! Having just finished the Seven Years War, the British were very suspicious of France, and military officers were frequently given secret orders so that details would not fall into the wrong hands. The secret orders given to Cook stated:

There is reason to imagine that a Continent of land of great extent may be found southward … you are to proceed southward in order to make discovery of the Continent … if you discover the Continent … you are to reemploy yourself diligently in exploring as great an extent of the coast as you can. You are also with the consent of the Natives to take possession of Convenient Situations in the Country, in the name of the King of Great Britain; or if you find the Country uninhabited take Possession for His Majesty by setting up Proper Marks and Inscriptions as first discoverers and Possessors.

Left: Statue of Captain Cook. *Right:* Box made from the wood of Captain Cook's ship, the *Endeavour*.

EMPTY CLAIMS

Cook did not claim possession of New Holland for Britain at Botany Bay, although he did hoist the Union Jack each day on shore, to the bewilderment of the Aborigines. He dropped anchor in Botany Bay on 29 April 1770, but it wasn't until 22 August 1770 that he raised the British flag and claimed "the whole Eastern Coast … by the name of New South Wales" at a place named Possession Island. In doing so, Cook made a grave error. He claimed the land as *terra nullius*, or land belonging to no-one — a decision that causes much offence and has had long-lasting ramifications for the Indigenous people of Australia, with whom no treaty has ever been agreed to. Cook's decision to claim the land as *terra nullius* was against the secret orders he had received. His orders instructed him to claim land only with "the consent of the natives". Banks later justified his captain's decision, writing in his journal:

> *We only once saw as many as thirty Indians* [all natives at the time were referred to as Indians] *together. We saw indeed only the sea coast; what the immense tracts of inland country may produce is to us totally unknown: we may have liberty to conjecture, however, that they are totally uninhabited.*

Above: The singing ship memorial at Emu Park, Queensland, is one of many tributes to Cook around the continent.

LEAVING TAHITI, the *Endeavour* first reached New Zealand and navigated the north and south islands before heading west to the east coast of New Holland. Point Hicks was the first land sighted and from there, heading north up the east coast, Cook named Cape Howe, Mount Dromedary and Batemans Bay. On 29 April, the *Endeavour* pulled into a sheltered bay and landed in the place now named Kurnell. Cook and his men explored Botany Bay, found shy inhabitants there, and scoured the headland opposite (now called La Perouse) for several days, carving the date and the ship's name into a tree to mark their landing. The ship continued north. Along the way, Cook named Port Jackson, Cape Byron, Queensland's Glass House Mountains and Bustard Bay, near the town of 1770.

A FOTHERING BOTHER

On 11 June 1770, the *Endeavour* struck the Great Barrier Reef, forcing a subsequent delay at Endeavour River to repair the vessel's badly damaged hull. The crew tried all sorts of remedies to drag the ship off the reef. Anything in the hold that wasn't essential was thrown overboard, including ballast, cannons and rotten food. Crew members used the row boats and anchor cable to try to tow the ship off the reef and the pumps were used continuously.

EVENTUALLY, the *Endeavour* was dragged off the reef at high tide with a lump of coral broken off in her hull. She was leaking badly and was salvaged only by the process of fothering — running a sail covered in chopped wool and animal dung underneath the ship so that the water pressure would suck it up to fill the hole. Seven weeks were then spent repairing the ship in the camp at Endeavour River, during which time the crew interacted with the Guugu-Yimidhirr Aboriginal people. Cook wrote about them in his journal:

> *… they could easily repeat many words after us, but neither us or Tupia could understand one word they said.*

Below: Kurnell, near Botany Bay.

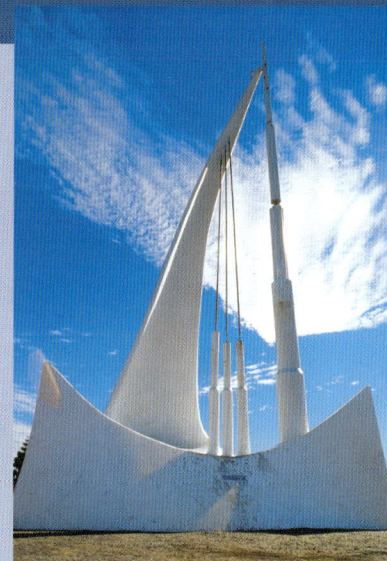

the FACTS!

COOK BROUGHT A TAHITIAN priest named Tupia with him to Australia. It was thought that Tupia would act as an interpreter for any people they met. Of course, he was not able to interpret or understand the language of any of the Australian Indigenous people they encountered any more than the British could.

THE ONLY PERSON on board to have used the technique of fothering previously was a young midshipman named Jonathan Monkhouse.

ISAAC SMITH, one of the *Endeavour*'s midshipmen and the cousin of Cook's wife, was the first European to set foot on the east coast. Cook is reported to have said to him, "Isaac, you shall land first".

THE AMERICAN WAR of Independence broke out in 1775 and occupied British forces until 1783. Further exploration of New South Wales was the least of their concerns for some years.

Above: On his journey north, Cook named the Glass House Mountains in Queensland.

What's in a name?
— places of their passage

This continent was known by many names until it was officially called Australia in writing by Governor Lachlan Macquarie in 1817. Today, throughout the continent, place names are a lasting reminder of the struggles and successes of exploration.

the FACTS!

CARSTENSZ NAMED Coen River after Jan Pieterszoon Coen — at the time the governor-general of the East Indies.

IN 1699, William Dampier named Shark Bay (below) after spotting many sharks in the waters near there. Many Australian place names now commemorate Dampier.

IN 1821, Captain Phillip Parker King named the Buccaneer Archipelago north of Broome after William Dampier, the "buccaneer" who sailed through it in 1688.

BOTANY BAY was at first called Stingray Bay, because of the many stingrays seen there. Once Banks realised the botanical wealth of the area, it was renamed Botany Bay.

TOP END EXPLORER John Lort Stokes named King Sound in 1838 after explorer Captain Phillip Parker King.

Europeans initially referred to the area south of New Guinea as *Terra Australis Incognita*, which is Latin for the "unknown southern land".

WITH DUTCH DISCOVERIES, parts were termed "New Holland", "Eendrachtsland", "Dedelsland", "Arnhem Land" and "De Witt's Land", while the English preferred "New South Wales". Carl Linnaeus was so overwhelmed by the sheer wealth of flora observed by botanist Joseph Banks that he suggested it should be called "Banksia"! In the end, it was navigator Matthew Flinders who proposed the name Australia. Later discoveries by the French added Gallic names to the list of localities — Peron Peninsula, D'Entrecasteaux National Park, Recherche Bay. Some explorers have as many as 30 places named in their honour!

Above: Melbourne's Flinders Street Station is named in honour of Matthew Flinders.

Above: Cook named Cape Tribulation "because here began all our troubles".

SOME NAMES hint at the frustration or joy of navigators, others pay tribute to wealthy patrons who funded the explorations — some commemorate voyagers who never set foot on Australian soil. Luis Vaez de Torres missed out on finding a continent, but that doesn't mean he didn't make a name for himself. At least seven Australian locations are named after Torres. Tasman bypassed the mainland, but gave his name to more than 30 places. On his journey north, Cook named numerous locations, including Port Jackson, Broken Bay, Port Stephens and Moreton Bay, which was named "Morton Bay" after the Earl of Morton, the President of the Royal Society, but was later misspelt. In Cook's honour, many Australian towns commemorate his voyage.

Left: A memorial to Captain Cook in the town that bears his name — Cooktown.

Above: The flat, shrubby Western Australian coastline near Shark Bay, which most of the early Dutch explorers chanced upon, contained no fresh water and was met with Dutch derision.

First impressions
in their own words

High hopes of a rich land were dashed when early explorers landed on the west coast. Most were unimpressed by the arid, destitute areas. Only with the discovery of arable land in the south and east did more flattering reports emerge.

THE DUTCH WERE UNFORTUNATE in that many of their investigations, both intentional and accidental, occurred in a largely featureless area of Western Australia. Dutch traders, who were making a lot of money out of the lush, spice-rich islands of Indonesia, considered their new finds a great disappointment. Willem Jansz was the first to conclude that "there was no good to be done there". Dampier, an Englishman used to greener pastures, found the harsh landscape distasteful and barren and the people "the miserablest people in the world". Had they seen the pastoral lands of the east coast or the verdant forests of the Victorian coastline, their judgement of the new land might have been entirely different.

Above: Tasman was impressed with the land he found around Adventure Bay, Tasmania.

OF THE DUTCH CONTINGENT, only Tasman's first impressions of the land were in any way favourable. He wrote:

> It is impossible to conceive a Country that promises fairer from its Situation than this of Terra Australis; no longer incognita, as this Map demonstrates, but the Southern Continent Discovered. It lies Precisely in the richest Climates of the World …

However, the lack of readily exploitable merchandise meant the Dutch East India Company decided not to act further on his investigations.

JAMES COOK, landing on the east coast, remarked that the land was not the "barren and Miserable Country that Dampier and others have described the Western Side to be". In several places along the mainland coast he recorded that the land was "thickly cloathed with wood"; however, the object was to chart the coast and few landings were made to explore the land they saw.

the FACTS!

JAN CARSTENSZ WROTE a very grim account of Australia, which he believed to be, *"the most arid and barren region that could be found anywhere on the earth"*.

ON 2 DECEMBER 1642, Tasman sent small boats to *"a bay situated north-west of us upwards of a mile's distance … the boats came back, bringing various samples of vegetables, which they had seen growing there in great abundance, some of them in appearance not unlike a certain plant growing at [the Cape of Good Hope] and fit to be used as pot-herbs …"*

COOK NOTED in his journal that the sandstone around Botany Bay (above) seemed *"very proper for building"*. He also saw *"a very fine stream of fresh water … on the north shore …"* and that *"wood for fuel may be got everywhere"*.

"THE LAND is of a dry sandy Soil, destitute of Water, except you make Wells …"* Dampier observed. "[Trees] are about the bigness of our large Apple-trees, and about the same height … There was pretty long Grass growing under the Trees; but it was very thin. We saw no Trees that bore fruit or berries."*

ON LEAVING Australia, Cook wrote that the land was still, *"in a pure state of Nature"* and that he thought *"most sorts of Grain, Fruits, Roots etc of every kind would flourish …"*

Above: Sir Joseph Banks (1743–1820).

the FACTS!

JOSEPH BANKS was wealthy and intelligent, but he was no fuddy-duddy. He got a tattoo from natives in Tahiti and he also penned the first written records of surfing!

BANKS AND SOLANDER together identified more than 3600 plant species and took more than 30,000 floral specimens back to England with them.

SOLANDER HAD STUDIED under the famed Swedish botanist Carl Linnaeus, the "father of binomial nomenclature".

WHEN THE CREW first returned to England, Banks, rather than Cook, was at first considered the hero of the journey and even King George II requested to meet him.

COMTE DE LA PÉROUSE, intrepid French explorer, also took a large team of artists, zoologists, botanists and mineralogists on board his two ships, the *Astrolabe* and the *Boussole*.

ON RETURNING TO ENGLAND, Banks employed five artists to engrave and paint the many preserved plant specimens he had brought back with him. The work was not completed in Banks' lifetime.

CHARLES GREEN travelled on board the *Endeavour* to record the transit of Venus in the Pacific. He was later made Astronomer Royal.

Men of science
— the naturalists

The 18th century was a time of great scientific enlightenment in Europe. Learned botanists, hydrographers, astronomers and zoologists formed powerful groups, such as the Royal Society, which influenced governments and championed research.

Countries, especially France and England, competed with each other for the prize of scientific knowledge, and esteemed men of science were frequently enlisted to help solve navigational and medical queries. As a result, naturalists began to be included on the muster list of exploratory voyages.

OF THEM, arguably the most famous is Sir Joseph Banks. He provided £10,000 of his own money to the *Endeavour* expedition and wrote in his journal:

> *Dr Solander and myself shall have probably greater opportunity in the course of this voyage than anyone has had before us … to add considerable Light to the Science which we so eagerly pursue.*

HOWEVER, BANKS WAS NOT the first scientist to set sail for the Great Southern Land. That honour goes to Louis de Bougainville (himself an excellent mathematician) whose ships sailed into the Pacific in 1768 with the first scientific crew on board, including renowned French astronomer Pierre-Antoine Véron and botanist and physician Philibert Commerçon.

Above: Scientific debate and discovery abounded as men of learning sought to understand the natural world. The painting above, created by John Hamilton Mortimer, shows (from left to right) Dr Daniel Solander, Sir Joseph Banks, Captain James Cook, Dr John Hawkesworth and the Earl of Sandwich. *Inset above:* Scarlet Banksia (*Banksia coccinea*).

Tributes in taxonomy

Some animals' scientific names identify the person who first recorded their existence, such as the Burrowing Bettong (*Bettongia lesueurii*) and Peron's Tree-frog (*Litoria peronii*).

AN EYE FOR DETAIL

When reports of the scientific finds of Banks and Solander surfaced in Europe, the French, now blossoming under the command of Napoleon Bonaparte, were eager to add their scientists and adventurers to the annals of history. Even the ship names of Nicolas Baudin's 1800 expedition — *Le Géographe* and *Le Naturaliste* — leave little doubt that France's mission was expected to be one of much scientific worth.

NO EXPENSE WAS SPARED in furnishing Baudin's expedition. Captain Baudin only wanted eight non-crew members with him per ship, but many well-to-do French families wanted their sons and nephews to be part of this important expedition that had Bonaparte's personal blessing. Eventually, Baudin took with him 24 astronomers, botanists, hydrographers, artists, zoologists and gardeners; to accommodate their needs, his ships even had libraries and water distillation plants on board! When the *Géographe* finally sailed, it had a full complement of 118 men. The *Naturaliste* sailed with 120 men — overcrowding was a serious problem. Two of the most famous scientists on board were Louis de Freycinet, a talented cartographer and surveyor, and François Péron, the first zoologist to visit Australia. Péron's discoveries led him to later question why Australia's unique animals had evolved. He pre-empted work on species origin, later brought to light by Charles Darwin, in suggesting that the different climate and environment had affected the animals' body types. Péron had a superb eye for detail, which was made even more remarkable for the fact that he only had one eye!

Right: François Péron — the first zoological expert on Australian soil. He amassed more than 100,000 Australian animal species.

AMATEUR ANTHROPOLOGISTS

Most naturalists were not just interested in plants and animals; they also wrote much about the people they met, and sometimes even took them home. Cook returned to England from his second journey with a young Tahitian boy named Omai.

JOSEPH BANKS and Cook had remained friends and Banks befriended the boy, took him in, garbed him in fine clothes and had him mingle in English high society — he even took Omai hunting in Yorkshire.

Left: Omai, Joseph Banks and Dr Solander.

the FACTS!

OF THE MANY learned men who undertook the voyage on Nicolas Baudin's ships, only seven saw out the journey.

ROBERT BROWN (shown in an engraving below) was the botanist on Matthew Flinders' journey. He was given the nickname "Jupiter Botanicus" because he was considered the "God" of plant identification.

BROWN AND HIS ASSISTANTS amassed a wealth of knowledge about the continent, collecting as many as 39,000 Australian species.

BROWN ALSO kept many records of the Aborigines and was the first person to call them "Australians", a name that would later be adopted for all residents of the country.

ALSO ON Flinders' *Investigator* were mineralogist John Allen and astronomer John Crosley.

LATER, naturalists and botanists such as Ferdinand von Mueller and Carl Lumholtz would similarly record the plants and animals of the inland, adding to the knowledge of natural history in Australia.

Above: Charles-Alexandre Lesueur (1778–1846).

the FACTS!

TEN OF NICOLAS BAUDIN'S scientific staff found life at sea too difficult and deserted when the ships reached the Ille de France (Mauritius). Baudin didn't care; he replaced them with two gifted young artists, Charles-Alexandre Lesueur (above) and Nicolas-Martin Petit, and wrote of the deserters, "*I hope that the result of the expedition will confirm my observation … that they were not necessary*".

NICOLAS-MARTIN PETIT actually came on board as an assistant gunner, but he was also a talented illustrator.

TWO ARTISTS ABOARD the *Endeavour*, Sydney Parkinson and Alexander Buchan, were helped by Swede, Herman Sporing, who was employed as a secretary but was also a fine sketcher.

SOME ARTISTS recorded animals that have since become extinct. The dwarf Kangaroo Island Emu (*Dromaius baudinianus*, below), once inhabited Kangaroo Island in South Australia. This painting by Lesueur now forms part of the limited biological information about this species.

Art of a new land
— illustrators & artists

Photography was yet to be invented, so the best record of the locations, animals, plants and people encountered was made by skilled artists, recreating detail from samples that the naturalists collected.

Beautiful, intricately detailed works depict all manner of plants, animals and landscapes. Some naturalists were not only expert botanists or zoologists but also accomplished artists; others employed talented men such as Charles-Alexandre Lesueur, William Westall, Sydney Parkinson and Alexander Buchan to reproduce sketches, engravings or paintings of the remarkable things they had found.

SOME WERE SPECIALIST landscape artists, such as William Westall; others tried their hand at just about anything, from dainty wildflowers to reptiles, insects and mammals. Many of them turned out a prolific body of work. Ferdinand Bauer, an Austrian artist on Flinders' voyage, created artwork of more than 1000 plants and 200 animals.

Above: This realistic depiction of quolls in Tasmania was created by naturalist Péron's artists on the Baudin 1800–03 expedition.

SIR SYDNEY PARKINSON

Banks was aided in his botanical documentation by the talented young Scottish-born artist Sydney Parkinson, who made the first visual record of the kangaroo and illustrated numerous plant species.

Parkinson's well-written journal details his account of the meeting with Aborigines in Botany Bay, after which he drew the first British portrait of Australian Aborigines, known as *Two of the Natives of New Holland, Advancing to Combat* (right).

Portraits of Australia

Artists made illustrations of birds, mammals, plants and other oddities they found on this continent.

VISTAS OF THE NEW LAND

At just nineteen years of age, William Westall boarded the *Investigator* to begin a journey that would lead to his renown. He was the landscape artist on Flinders' voyage and, although his English sensibilities often recoiled at the harsh landscape, his evocative artwork captures the beauty and sparsity of Australian environments. Although specifically employed as a landscape artist, Westall could also competently draw animals, as his depiction of a snake (opposite) demonstrates. He was also the first person to copy figures seen in Aboriginal rock art.

Above: Self-portrait of William Westall (1781–1850).

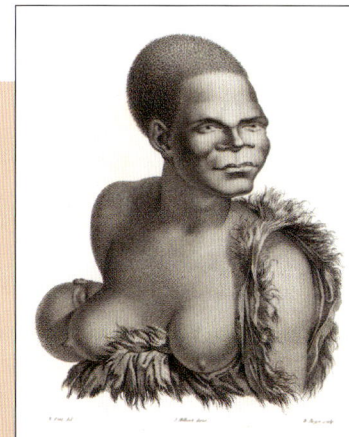

Above: Nicolas-Martin Petit's illustration of Arra-Maida, a Tasmanian Aboriginal woman and her child, records a tribe now believed to be extinct.

Above: Robert Westall, William Westall's son, recreated this scene from of one of his father's paintings showing the rugged landscape seen from the summit of Mount Westall, Queensland.

FOLLOWING IN THEIR FOOTSTEPS

Within just a few years, a young midshipman who had come to the new colony aboard the First Fleet would continue the artistic work begun so beautifully by Parkinson, Westall and others. George Raper was barely out of his teens when he arrived in Sydney, but he had a natural gift for illustration. Along with other artists of the fledgling colony, he made illustrations of birds, plants and flowers. George Caley and John William Lewin also created superb illustrations of Australia's fauna and flora.

Right: J.W. Lewin's depiction of a pair of Galahs.

the FACTS!

ARTIST GEORGE STUBBS made the first painting of a kangaroo in 1772, basing it on sketches (below) made by Sydney Parkinson. He may even have stuffed a kangaroo skin that Banks brought back to use as a model.

SYDNEY PARKINSON drew at least 1300 intricately detailed sketches before he contracted dysentery and died at sea in 1771.

THE ARTWORK of natural historian La Billardiere, the artist on Bruny d'Entrecasteaux's voyage, was stolen by the English when the vessel was captured during the French Revolution. Joseph Banks later persuaded the English to return the artwork to France.

Above: An Aborigine preparing a fire.

the FACTS!

DAMPIER MOST LIKELY came into contact with the Bardi or Djawi peoples of Australia's north-west.

JAN CARSTENSZ agreed to pay his men eight pieces of gold if they captured an Aborigine. Near the Coen River on Cape York, they kidnapped a man from either the Wik or Kantju tribe — of course this angered the Aborigines!

DAMPIER at first attempted to befriend the Karajarri Aborigines, but when his efforts failed he turned to kidnapping, which led to violence. One of Dampier's crew was speared in the cheek and Dampier shot at and wounded an Aboriginal man.

COOK MADE A COMMENT on entering Botany Bay that seemed to pre-empt the feelings of the Aboriginal people in relation to the coming of the Europeans, "… all they seem'd to want was for us to be gone", wrote Cook.

IN 1801, William Bowen (on Murray's expedition along the Victorian coast) met with Aborigines who insisted that he and his party remove their clothes. They did so and were met with wonder at the colour of their skin; the Aborigines then turned to Bowen and made "significant signs that he must have washed himself very hard".

CAPTAIN COOK WROTE in his journal on 22 August 1770 of not one, but many sightings of Indigenous inhabitants around Botany Bay and the islands: *"…we expected they would have opposed our landing but as we approached the Shore they made off and left us in peaceable possession of as much of the Island as served our purpose".*

Friend or foe?
— the people they found

We can only imagine how alarmed Aborigines must have been by the influx of white men with guns. Understandably, their interactions with the white invaders fluctuated from curiosity, to friendliness, to avoidance and, occasionally, to violence.

Above: A rendition of Cook's first approach to Botany Bay in 1770, showing the two proud Aborigines who were resolved to oppose his landing.

As with the landscape, the "natives", too, received very poor press from the early adventurers. Carstensz labelled them "utter barbarians" and Dampier wrote a very unflattering account of the peoples he encountered, suggesting:

The inhabitants of this country are the miserablest people in the world … [they] have no Houses, and skin Garments, Sheep, Poultry and Fruits of the Earth, Ostrich Eggs, & c. … setting aside their humane shape, they differ but little from brutes … They have no sort of clothes; but a piece of the rind of a tree tied like a girdle about their waists, and a handful of long grass, or three or four small green boughs full of leaves, thrust under their girdle to cover their nakedness.

CREATING CONFLICT

Most explorers failed to see themselves as invaders and were perplexed that the Aborigines placed little value on housing, clothes or wealth. Jan Carstensz, especially, made the mistake of evaluating the land and its people on European terms, expecting the Aborigines to be able to tell him about minerals and manufacturing! He wrote:

In spite of all our kindness … the blacks received us as enemies everywhere … nor could we get any information [about] towns and villages … the land … the religion … what manufactures, what minerals, whether gold, silver, tin, iron, lead, copper or quicksilver.

Above: Aborigines enjoyed a simple existence in a land that provided a pleasant climate and plentiful food, if one knew where to find it. The explorers did not understand the Aborigines' lifestyle, labelling them "barbarians", "savages" and "brutes".

Above: Face and body painting was common.

LATER, COOK also ran into trouble when he tried to land at Botany Bay. "I went in the boats in hopes of speaking with them …", he wrote, "… as we approached the shore they all made off except two men who seemed resolved to oppose our landing". Captain Cook fired at the men, but the two brave Aborigines still refused to let him land. At first they threw a stone at the ship and then launched their spears.

IN CONTRAST, the Guugu-Yimidhirr people of the Endeavour River made friends with Cook's crew — despite the Europeans' breaches of etiquette and inability to see that clothes and trinkets meant little to these simple-living people. Banks recorded:

Cloth, nails, paper and such were given them…all which they took and put in the canoe without showing the least sign of satisfaction: at last a small fish was by accident thrown them on which they expressed the greatest joy imaginable…

LATER, THE ABORIGINES POLITELY brought a fish in return. The British did not return this favour. On 19 July, the crew caught several large turtles. The Guugu-Yimidhirr visited the campsite, requesting their rightful share of the food caught on their lands — two of the turtles. Unfortunately, the British, having 90 mouths to feed, refused. In retaliation, some of the Aborigines set fire to grass around the campsite and were chased and shot at by the crew. Later, a Guugu-Yimidhirr elder came to make

peace with the sailors, bringing a spear with no spearhead to show he considered the fight over.

EVENTUALLY, COOK seemed to grasp the truth behind the Aborigines' simple existence, writing:

They lie in a Tranquillity which is not disturbed by the Inequality of Condition; the Earth and the Sea of their own accord furnished them with all the things necessary for life, they … live in a warm and fine Climate and enjoy a very wholesome Air. In short, they seemed to set no Value upon anything we gave them … this in my opinion argues that they think themselves provided with all the necessities of life and that they have no superfluities.

Nicolas Baudin also sympathised, writing to Governor King:

I have never been able to conceive that there was justice or even fairness on the part of the Europeans in seizing, in the name of their governments, a land seen for the first time, when it is inhabited by men who have not always deserved the title of savages or cannibals that has been given them …"

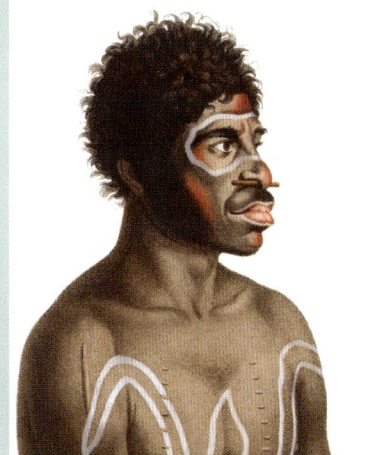

the FACTS!

ONE ABORIGINE, whom Dampier thought must be a kind of prince, had, "*a circle of white paste or pigment (a sort of lime as we thought it) about his eyes and a white streak down his nose from his forehead to the tip of it*".

THE EORA PEOPLE lived to the north of Botany Bay and the Tharawal people to the south.

AFTER THE TURTLE INCIDENT, Banks discovered some of the clothing given to the Aborigines discarded in the bush. He wrote, "*… they seemed to set no value upon any thing we had except our turtle, which of all things we were the least able to spare them*".

ONCE, FRANÇOIS PÉRON (the man believed to have coined the term "anthropologist"), and a companion chanced upon a group of Aboriginal women on a fishing expedition. To show the women they were friendly, they danced for them. In return the women offered to paint the Frenchmen's faces and Péron agreed, in the *"interests of Science"*. He later remarked that *"they looked on us with satisfaction, seemingly complimenting us on our additional charms"*.

Above: Waratah flower.

An island rich in
floral splendour

Australia's geographic isolation made it a biological wonderland, filled with plant species that had evolved largely independently since the break-up of Gondwana. Naturalists and botanists were astounded by the floral diversity they found.

While the raw Western Australian coast offered little in the way of floral splendour, Botany Bay, Tasmania and the east coast proved a different matter. The entire east coast was rich in plant life. Over the course of the three-year voyage from 1768–71, Banks and Solander collected approximately 30,000 species — almost one-third of these were native to Australia and previously unrecorded.

the
FACTS!

UNBEKNOWNST TO the explorers, Indigenous peoples used the flowering of certain plants as a calendar to determine when particular food sources would be the most plentiful. The Tharawal people of south Sydney knew that when the lilly pilly fruit began to drop, they had to prepare for winter. Similarly, Tasmanian Aborigines knew that flowering bloodwoods heralded the arrival of the muttonbirds.

EVEN THE DESOLATE, coarse red sandhills surrounding Shark Bay (below) bloom with flowers at certain times of the year.

PARKINSON wrote in his journal that at Botany Bay they found, "*a variety of flowering shrubs; a tree that yields gum; and a species of palm* [Borasus flabellifer]*, the berries of which are of two sorts; one small, eaten by the hogs, and the other as large as a cherry, has a stone in it; it is of a pale crimson colour, and has the taste of sweet acid. We also found a species of* Salvia fortea".

PARKER KING also noted that *Casuarina paludosa* was "*abundant in the swamps and low grounds at Port Jackson, where the colonists call it the 'Swamp Oak'*".

DRAGON-TREES
AND TALL TIMBER

Dampier referred to gum trees as "dragon trees" because of the red "blood" (sap) that was seen oozing from their bark. He wrote:

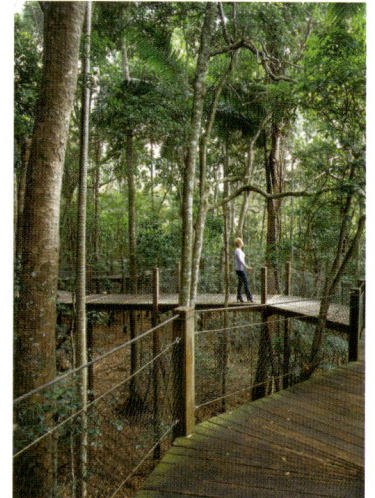

Most of the Trees that we saw are Dragon-Trees ... and these too are the largest trees of any there. They are about the bigness of our large Apple-trees, and about the same heighth [sic]… the Gum distils out of the Knots or Cracks that are in the Bodies of the Trees. We compared it with some Gum-Dragon or Dragon's Blood that was aboard, and it was of the same colour and taste.

PHILLIP PARKER KING, in surveying parts of the east coast from 1818–22, carefully described the subtropical rainforest he found around Port Macquarie, writing:

The trichillia and the ficus, before noted, are abundant on these banks, and are all intricately connected with each other by climbing plants, which grow to an incredible size, and hang down in rich clusters from the summit to the root of the tree, tending considerably to beautify the richness of the scene.

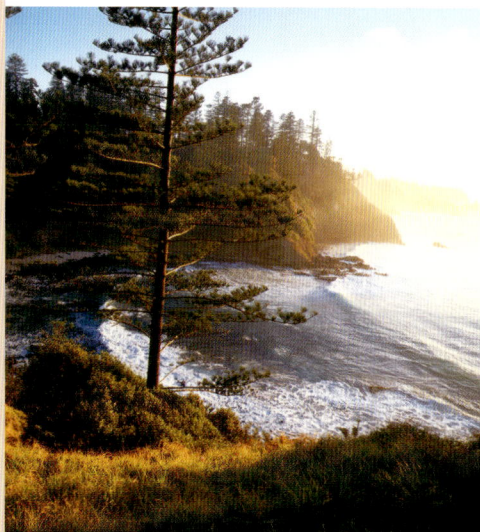

PART OF THE ATTRACTION of a settlement at Norfolk Island was the tall, straight Norfolk Pine (left), which, unfortunately for Governor King, was too heavily knotted to be of much use in ship building. Van Diemen's Land was blessed with the much more useful Huon Pine, but still Australia's lush rainforests and Mountain Ash forests went undiscovered until a wider exploration of the inland could be made. When Europeans first stumbled across these incredible pockets of wilderness, they found the tallest flowering trees on Earth — the Mountain Ash.

Art imitating life

George Raper's illustration of Native Fuchsia (*Epacris longiflora*) appears almost identical to a photograph taken of the same plant.

BUSH TUCKER

Despite a few "pot-herbs", most early explorers failed to utilise edible plant species. At the Endeavour River, Cook's men benefited from "Purslain and beans, which grows on a Creeping kind of Vine. The first [they] found very good when boiled, and the latter not to be despised". Had the explorers known more about "bush tucker" they might have found certain plant species more to their liking. Cook wrote:

The Land naturally produces hardly anything fit for Man to eat, and the Natives know nothing of Cultivation. There are, indeed, growing wild in the wood a few sorts of Fruit (the most of them unknown to us), which when ripe do not eat amiss, one sort especially, which we called Apples, being about the size of a Crab Apple it is black and pulpey when ripe, and tastes like a Damson, it hath a large, hard stone or kernel, and grows on Trees or Shrubs.

RECORDING SPECIMENS

Botanists pressed many specimens to take back to England, where talented artists set about illustrating the petals, stems, leaves and fruit in great detail. Banks alone collected so many specimens that his Florilegium, a collection of 743 floral images engraved and painted on copper plates, was not completed during his lifetime. In fact, the British Museum produced the first limited edition only in 1984, publishing 738 plates. A more immediate record was made by artists in the field, and many of the early artworks are superbly detailed.

Above: Naturalists and artists made excellent representations of Australian flora. William Westall's portrayal of a grass-tree near Port Jackson (right) bears up well against a photograph taken in the Flinders Ranges (left). Aborigines used the floral spikes of this plant to make spears.

the FACTS!

A FEMALE CONVICT wrote home to England that in the penal colony at Sydney Cove, "*Something like Ivy is used for tea*". She was probably talking about the Native Sarsaparilla plant (*Smilax glycophylla*), which was used to keep scurvy at bay.

PREVENTING SCURVY required fresh fruit or vegetables and Banks identified some native plant species that could be eaten, including figs, palm-tree cabbage, purslain and "*a Kind of Beans, very bad, a kind of Parsley and a plant something resembling spinage* [spinach]".

BOTANISTS kept specimens carefully preserved by pressing them between the pages of special books or keeping them folded in damp cloth. The specimen below is one that Sir Joseph Banks took back to England with him.

WHEN THE *ENDEAVOUR* was being repaired at the Endeavour River, Cook wrote, "*The best greens we found here was the Tarra* [Taro]".

TASMAN AND HIS CREW collected and ate "sea parsley", which was probably *Apium prostratum*, or wild celery.

Below: Rainbow Lorikeets.

Unique fauna
of a new continent

Australia's superbly adapted animals perplexed and amazed newcomers to these shores. Mammals, reptiles and birds were described with astonishment, but often incorrectly assumed to be strange versions of species that were already recorded to science.

the FACTS!

SYDNEY PARKINSON wrote in his journal that near Botany Bay they found "*two sorts of parroquets* [sic], *and a beautiful loriquet* [sic]: *we shot a few of them, which we made into a pie, and they ate very well*".

BANKS SHOT an animal that he described as "like a greyhound" near the Endeavour River. He heard the Guugu people call it a word that sounded like "kanguroo". Later, when settlers enquired about "kanguroos" near Botany Bay, the Aborigines appeared not to understand. It took some time for the British to learn that Australian Aborigines spoke many distinctly different languages.

COOK'S JOURNAL records, "*Besides the Animals which I have before mentioned, called by the Natives Kangooroo, or Kanguru, here are Wolves, Possums, an Animal like a ratt* [sic], *and snakes, both of the venomous and other sorts. Tame animals here are none except Dogs, and of these we never saw but one*".

WHEN JOHN THISTLE, a crew mate and friend of Matthew Flinders, caught a large snake on shore, he sewed its mouth shut and took it on board for the scientists to examine and draw.

SPECIES OF POSSUM, being widespread over much of the continent, were among the first to be described by Captain Cook's crew and on subsequent voyages around the new colony. Early explorers believed them to be opossums, similar to the South American species. Many elongated depictions made by naturalists, showing the possum (right) on the ground rather than in the trees, do them little justice.

Above: Emus, or the "Australian Ostrich", were hunted for food and their eggs were prized.

OF ALL THE ANIMALS encountered, birds alone seemed akin to those the explorers had found in other parts of the world, with the exception of a great many parrots and some other species never before recorded. William Dampier made detailed drawings of noddies and other sea birds and published them in his book, *A Voyage to New Holland.* Dampier probably also made the first sighting of the iconic Sulphur-crested Cockatoo, writing of "a sort of white parrot, which flew a great many together."

DINGOES were often glimpsed, and frequently mistaken for wolves. "My men saw two or three beasts like hungry wolves, lean like so many skeletons, being nothing but skin and bones," wrote Dampier, giving an excellent description of the naturally thin Dingo (below). Dutch navigator, Willem de Vlamingh mentioned that some of his party had "seen a yellow dog jump out of the scrub and throw itself into the sea as if to enjoy a swim".

Faunal phenomena

Near Broad Sound, north Queensland, Banks discovered "millions of butterflies", ants, interesting plant specimens and "the very singular Phaenomenon [sic]" of the mudskipper, which travelled over dry land.

CAT, MOUSE OR MARSUPIAL?

Francisco Pelsaert, commander of the wrecked *Batavia*, was the first European to describe one of Australia's many macropod species. Pelsaert was amazed by these "creatures of miraculous form", which he took to be "numbers of a species of cat". He made the first observation that they suckled their young in a pouch, noting:

Bellow the belly the female carries a pouch, into which you may put your hand; inside the pouch are her nipples, and we have found that the young ones grow up in this pouch with the nipples in their mouths. We have seen some young ones lying there which were only the size of a bean, though at the same time perfectly proportioned, so that it seems certain that they grow there out of the nipples …

PELSAERT WAS WRONG on the last count, but his description is still a remarkably good record of tiny pouch young. Forty-five years later, Willem de Vlamingh would mistake another of these marsupials for a rodent! De Vlamingh named Rottnest Island after this "rat as large as a common cat", which was actually the stout little marsupial Quokka. Cook and the men that followed him expressed a similar fascination with kangaroos, likening them to a greyhound in size and speed, although both Cook and Banks also recorded in their journals that the kangaroo bore little resemblance to any European animal. Flinders, upon finding Kangaroo Island, made a feast of "half a hundredweight of heads, forequarters and tails … stewed down into soup for dinner on this and the succeeding days".

Right: Willem de Vlamingh mistook the Quokka for a type of large rat.

REVERSE LIZARDS

The Shingleback lizard disgusted William Dampier, who described it as:

… a sort of iguana … differing from [others] in 3 remarkable particulars: for these had a larger and uglier head, and had no tail: and at the Rump, instead of the Tail there, they had a Stump of a Tail which appeared like another Head; but not really such, being without Mouth or Eyes: Yet this creature seemed by this Means to have a Head at each End … the legs also seem'd all 4 of them to be Forelegs … and seeming by the Joints and Bending to be made as if they were to go indifferently either Head or Tail foremost. They were speckled black and yellow like toads, and had Scales or Knobs on their Backs like those of Crocodiles, plated onto the Skin … They are very slow in Motion; and when a man comes Nigh … will stand still and hiss, not endeavouring to get away. Their livers are also spotted black and yellow: and the body when opened has a very unsavoury smell. I did never see such ugly creatures anywhere but here.

Above: Cook and his men feasted on a Bustard in north Queensland.

Above: Sir Thomas Mitchell lent his name to the pink cockatoos he found.

Above: Abundant fish, stingrays and turtles provided seafood for sailors.

Above: Tasman's crew had "observed certain footprints of animals, not unlike those of Tiger's claws", which were most likely the paw prints of the now-extinct Tasmanian Tiger.

Above: The First Fleet's flagship, HMS *Sirius*.

the FACTS!

WHEN THE FIRST FLEET sailed into Sydney Cove, Aboriginal people met them on the shore, shouting "Wurra Wurra", which means "Go away!" in the language of the local Aborigines.

THE SHIPS WERE NAMED HMS *Sirius*, HMS *Supply*, *Alexander*, *Lady Penrhyn*, *Charlotte*, *Prince of Wales*, *Scarborough*, *Friendship*, *Fishburn*, *Golden Grove* and the *Borrowdale*.

ALL OF THE SHIPS but the *Sirius* and the *Supply* were hastily unpacked and then set sail back to England, with some taking up a cargo of tea from Asia on the return journey.

MOST OF THE CONVICT women aboard were young, between 16 and 35 years of age. Several were pregnant and some children were born on the difficult journey.

AT FIRST, convicts lived in tents, but they were quickly put to work constructing more permanent dwellings. Huts were made of wattle-and-daub, which often collapsed in drenching rain.

OF THE PRISONERS, few had a trade background apart from five bricklayers, three plasterers, three carpenters, two cabinet-makers, one brickmaker, one blacksmith and a stonemason. Mortar for bricks was unavailable, so women collected oyster shells to be ground into lime for cement. Despite this, most brickwork failed to set properly and most of the early buildings collapsed!

The first fleet
— a colony of convicts

British interest in the newly acquired New South Wales stalled when Cook returned with reports that there was no "Great Southern Land". However, Britain's out-of-control criminal population drove Banks to suggest a colony at Botany Bay. Soon Britain's underprivileged, criminals, prostitutes and thieves would become settlers of a new land.

Eleven ships carrying more than 1400 people, including officials, passengers and crew, left Portsmouth for the new land on 13 May 1787. Eight months later, the weary seafarers and convicts took the first glimpse of their new home.

GOVERNOR ARTHUR PHILLIP quickly dismissed Botany Bay as a suitable place for a settlement. Instead, venturing north, he entered Sydney Heads and saw "the finest harbour in the world" — Port Jackson, now better known as Sydney Harbour. He examined the many coves and settled on one "that had the best spring of fresh water", naming it Sydney Cove after Viscount Sydney, the then Home Secretary of the British Government. Phillip then returned to the ships and had them all moved to Sydney Cove.

PHILLIP AND HIS SORRY BAND of prisoners, officers and marines were to be the first European explorers of the hinterland of Australia's east coast. But their first task was to establish buildings, storehouses, roads, vegetable gardens and other hallmarks of a settlement. The convicts and marines were ill-equipped and inexperienced for this task, but were put to work immediately, clearing bush and logging timber.

Above: Artist's impression of convicts in Britain being rowed out to the First Fleet's ships.

Below: On 26 January 1788, the Union Jack was raised and the marines and officers drank toasts to King George III, Queen Charlotte, the Prince of Wales and the success of the colony. This date is now celebrated as Australia Day.

Reliving history

Many re-enactments of the First Fleet entering Sydney Harbour have been made.

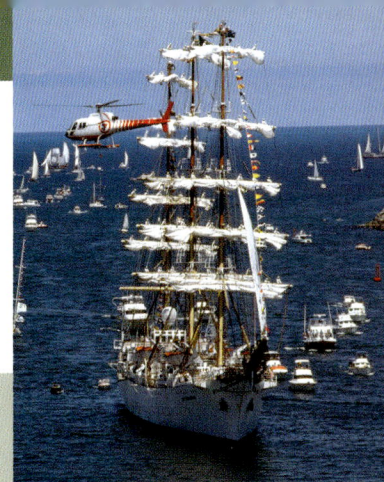

Above: A First Fleet re-enactment.

WITHIN FIVE WEEKS, Phillip began to undertake another task that had been entrusted to him — further exploration around the colony. In a long boat, he visited Broken Bay and discovered Brisbane Water. Rowing west of the settlement he found the mouth of the Hawkesbury River and later remarked on the "finest piece of water I ever saw" — he named it Pitt Water, after William Pitt, the prime minister of England, but it is now known as Pittwater. By April, he had travelled as far as Lake Narrabeen and noted "a very fine view of the mountains inland". These were the Blue Mountains, which surround the Sydney region and would later prove a frustrating obstacle to further exploration.

A WORTHY LEADER

Governor Phillip endeavoured to ensure fairness for all in the struggling colony. He was particularly mindful of the Aborigines:

I shall think it a great point gained if I can proceed … without having any great dispute with the natives; a few of them I shall endeavour to settle near us and whom I mean to furnish with everything that can tend to civilise them, and give them a high opinion of their new guests.

Phillip was the first to use Aboriginal guides and befriended many Aborigines over his time as governor. When he became ill after being speared by a hostile Aborigine at Manly, he returned to England, taking with him the Aborigines Bennelong and Yemmerawannie, who were introduced to the King of England.

Above: Governor Arthur Phillip (1738–1814) was well respected as a sensible, just man undertaking a very difficult task.

the FACTS!

PHILLIP was missing the tooth that the Aborigines traditionally pulled out in a manhood initiation ceremony — this seemed to help them trust him and relate to him.

IN HIS FIRST LETTER to Lord Sydney, Phillip wrote of his first meeting with the Aborigines: "*When I first landed at Botany Bay the natives appeared on the beach and were very easily persuaded to receive what was offered them and tho' they came armed, very readily returned the confidence I placed in them by going to them alone and unarmed, most of them laying down their spears when desired; and while the ships remained in Botany Bay no dispute happened upon our people and the natives*".

NAPOLEON BONAPARTE himself had applied to sail on La Pérouse's voyage in 1785 but was turned down. He later became Emperor.

AN UNEXPECTED GUEST

Soon after the First Fleet arrived, two 500-tonne French ships, the *Astrolabe* and the *Boussole*, sailed into Botany Bay. In 1785, Jean-François de Galaup La Pérouse (right), who greatly admired Captain Cook, was sent on a four-year assignment under the brief of France's Minister of the Marine, Comte de Fleurieu. He was instructed to complete a survey of the Pacific coasts of Asia and North America and the Pacific Islands. In order to make the necessary scientific observations, La Pérouse (1741-88) took with him a large team of artists, zoologists, botanists and mineralogists. Part of his mission was also to discern whether or not the landmass of New Holland was separated into large islands by inland channels. If it was, then France would have found suitable land to claim as their own. The *Astrolabe* carried engraved copper plates bearing the signs of French royalty in case such islands should be discovered. La Pérouse was nothing if not unlucky; his ships arrived in Botany Bay just six days after the First Fleet. His scientific team spent six weeks making new longboats and taking notes near Botany Bay before sailing off again.

Above: Depiction of convicts being deported.

the FACTS!

LIVESTOCK BROUGHT OUT included 122 chickens and 87 chicks; 35 ducks; 29 geese; 18 turkeys; 32 pigs; 44 sheep; 19 goats; 4 mares and 2 stallions; just 4 cows along with a bull and a bull calf; 5 rabbits; as well as kittens, puppies and greyhounds.

BY APRIL 1790, prisoners were actually starving to death. Supplies were so short that rations had to be halved and many did not survive on the weekly 1.1 kg of salt pork, 0.7 kg of rice or dried peas, and 1.8 kg of flour that was allocated.

PHILLIP HAD TO factor in the long delay in sending or receiving mail to London. With 24,000 km between London and Botany Bay, a letter took at least 15 months from when it was sent to the time a reply might arrive in Sydney.

AFTER THE *SIRIUS* was shipwrecked, the starving colony was left totally isolated when the *Supply* was sent to Batavia for food.

WORSE NEWS was that the HMS *Guardian*, which had been carrying supplies, was wrecked near the Cape of Good Hope and valuable, much needed supplies were lost.

THE FIRST SHIP of the Second Fleet arrived in June 1790, when the *Lady Juliana*, carrying 225 women and children, sailed into Sydney Cove. The existing convicts were not happy to have company. The ship carried hardly any supplies and a lot more hungry mouths to feed.

CONDITIONS ON BOARD the Second Fleet were terrible. Almost a quarter of the convicts transported died during the journey.

Life in a
strange new land

In the mistaken belief that the new colony would soon be self-sufficient, the First Fleet carried with it only enough provisions for the journey and for a subsequent two years. Deprivation, disease and starvation marred the colony's early years.

FOOD WAS A CONSTANT PROBLEM. Fish were plentiful, but Governor Phillip, noting that the Aborigines shared all of their food, rightfully decreed that a share of fish must be given to the Aborigines. There were few convicts with farming experience on board the First Fleet and they soon found that the sandy soils were quite unsuitable for growing vegetables or crops. The agriculture issue was compounded by the settlers planting seeds in the wrong season for the new climate and by the limited farming tools provided — a major oversight when the ships had left London. Women's clothes and ammunitions were also left off the list of provisions, so the marines soon ran low on firepower.

REWARD OR RUIN

Added to the woes of the colony was that it was comprised of convicts and petty criminals, who could hardly be expected to remain honest in the face of hardship. The aim was to reform convicts, but the harsh conditions led to many thefts.

TO ENCOURAGE good behaviour, convicts who worked hard and added to the colony's success were emancipated and rewarded with grants of land. Freed convicts were granted 30 acres, or 50 acres if they were married.

Marriage was encouraged because, with so many women of questionable morals in the colony, officers wanted to minimise the risk of promiscuity and prostitution.

JUDGES AND CONSTABLES were appointed to deal with those who refused to reform, and the first criminal court sat in session on 11 February 1788. The first to be tried was Samuel Barsby, who was sentenced to 150 lashes for assaulting a marine. Another convict, James Tennihill, who stole bread, was imprisoned on Pinchgut Island and given nothing but bread and water to eat for a week. The

Above: Tents were set up until more permanent dwellings could be established. By November 1788, a female convict wrote, "We now have two streets, if four rows of the most miserable huts you can possibly conceive of deserve that name …"

Working on the chain gang

Convicts in chains were led out to dig up fields to plant crops or hack down bush and create new "roads" for the settlement. It was hot, dusty, back-breaking work.

marines, all of whom had been volunteers and men of high morals when they set out from England, began to suffer from association with those of lesser character. They consumed much rum and were even accused of stealing supplies on occasion.

BY FEBRUARY 1790, a group of well-behaved convicts headed by John Harris persuaded Governor Phillip to make them watchmen, so they could watch over the colony's stores and prevent robberies. The watch system worked well, until Major Ross, the head of the marine corps, protested that it was "an insult to the corps of marines" to see convicts arrest his intoxicated soldiers.

WEST, NORTH AND TO NORFOLK

With the colony at Sydney Cove wracked by starvation, theft and disease, marines, officers and even Governor Phillip frequently searched for more suitable farming lands and other means of sustenance close to the new settlement.

MOVING INLAND, they discovered Farm Cove (Sydney's present-day botanic gardens) and Rose Hill, which was later renamed Parramatta — an Aboriginal word meaning "where the eels lie down". To the north, Manly Cove was named after the "confident and manly bearing" of the Aboriginal men Phillip met there.

TO PREVENT NORFOLK ISLAND (which Captain Cook had discovered in 1744) being settled by the French or another naval power, Phillip had instructions to settle it as soon as possible. On 14 February 1788, Lieutenant Phillip Gidley King sailed there to start a colony. He took with him six marines, an officer, two men to harvest the natural flax and tall Norfolk Pine, a surgeon, a midshipman and fifteen convicts. The small group settled at Arthurs Vale and began to fell the pine to make buildings. Both the Sydney and Norfolk penal colonies were to suffer a severe blow when the *Sirius* (above), transporting more convicts to Norfolk, was wrecked on a coral reef close to the island on 19 March 1790, leaving both colonies isolated. However, the colonies grew and by 1792 there were 1115 people on Norfolk — many of their descendants remain there today.

the FACTS!

ON 16 DECEMBER 1791, assistant surgeon John Irving became the colony's first freed convict.

CONVICTS LOOKED a little like bananas in prison pyjamas in their yellow and black uniforms (below) and strange rounded little caps.

AN ABORIGINE, Arabanoo, was captured by Phillip in the hope that he could tell the settlers how, or where, to find food. He later lived among the settlers and was highly respected. Arabanoo was known for his strength of character — Watkin Tench's journal reports that the gentle-tempered Arabanoo was proud and always refused to agree that the British were superior to him in any way — rightly so!

IN 1789, an epidemic of smallpox decimated the Aboriginal population of Sydney Cove. The Aborigines had no immunity to European diseases. The Eora people named the illness *galgalla*, which means "evil spirit".

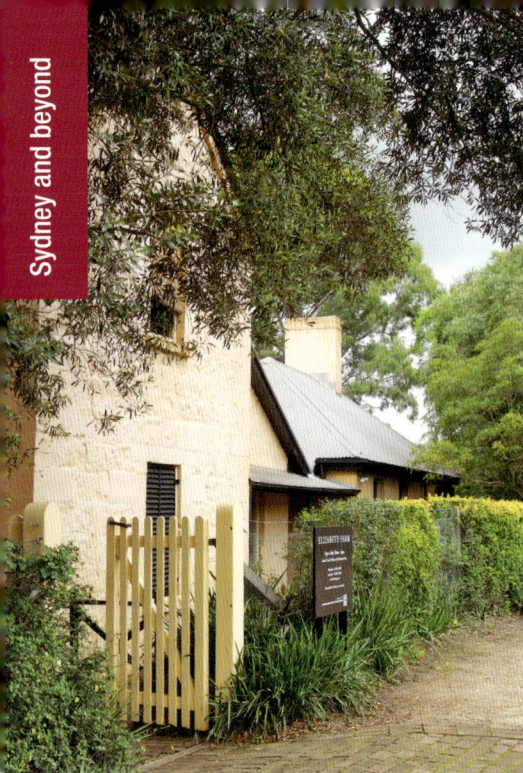

Rose Hill

Government House and many of the most established farms were at Rose Hill (now Parramatta).

Above: MacArthur's Elizabeth Farm in Rose Hill (1793) contains Australia's oldest standing building.

PROFIT FROM TOIL

The Sydney Cove and Norfolk Island colonies had a rocky start. It took many years for the new settlers to become self-sufficient; however, movement of settlers away from Sydney Cove, to land that was more suitable for farming, saw the colony spread out. The journey from Sydney Cove to the new region of Rose Hill (Parramatta) took about four hours by boat, but many of the settlers who had made the trip were making a good living out of farming their land. Governor Phillip even built his residence, Government House, at Rose Hill.

Above: The Rocks area, where Cadman's Cottage stands today, was first to be settled. Rose Hill followed.

Above: By the turn of the century, Sydney, painted in 1800 by convict artist Thomas Watley, was flourishing.

IN 1791, THE THIRD FLEET ARRIVED, increasing the population of the colony by approximately 1800 people, including members of the New South Wales Corps, who were intended to replace the marines and act as the colony's disciplinarians. Before the ships returned home they took to whaling, fast realising there was profit to be made in Australian waters. More whaling ships followed and the colony became a convenient place for American trading or whaling ships to sell their wares en route to China. Soon, the Sydney settlement began to grow and slowly prospered. By the time Governor Arthur Phillip, exhausted and in poor health, returned to England in 1792, settlers and officers who had survived the hard days began to vie for control of the colony. Under the command of Major Francis Grose, the corps resumed control until such time as a suitable governor could be appointed. Corruption and profiteering were to follow. In the absence of banknotes (which had also been overlooked), rum became the currency of the colony, and officers imported it and sold it at huge profit (as much as 1000%). By 1794, Grose had returned to England and left Captain William Paterson in charge. Like most of the head men of the Sydney settlement, Paterson explored the land surrounding the colony, but governors Captain John Hunter, Phillip Gidley King and William Blight, were soon appointed in succession to curb the corps' excesses. Each of them made further explorations around the colony and the coast.

Close to the colony
— exploration near Sydney

Not all of the marines were corrupt — one of them, the 31-year-old Captain Watkin Tench, explored the perimeters of the colony and left an interesting, humorous journal of his travels.

TENCH WAS NOT the only marine or officer to seek out adventures around Sydney Cove, but he was the one that perhaps best recorded his discoveries. Very little was known about the territory west of Parramatta, so in June 1789 Tench set out westward to further explore areas chanced upon earlier by Governor Phillip. In doing so, after a two-day march, he discovered the Nepean River (so named later by Governor Phillip), writing that they had landed themselves, "on the banks of a river, nearly as broad as the Thames at Putney, and apparently of great depth".

Above: **William Paterson (1755–1810) was Administrator of the New South Wales Corps from May 1794, but also explored near the colony.**

RIVERS DEEP, MOUNTAINS HIGH

The Sydney river system remained a great puzzle to Governor Phillip and the residents of the penal colony, who wanted to know whether the three discovered rivers — the Hawkesbury, Grose and Nepean — met and intersected or were three separate rivers.

Taking two Aboriginal guides, Phillip, who had just returned from rowing further along the Hawkesbury River, set out with 21 men to determine how Sydney's river system worked. Phillip failed in his endeavour, finding that the guides were little help and eventually giving up when the party reached a swiftly flowing creek they could not cross.

WATKIN TENCH and another marine officer, William Dawes, continued the research in May 1791, coming from a different direction that, as Tench wrote, "completely settled the long contested point about the Hawkesbury and Nepean … We found them to be one river". Tench and Dawes continued on towards the Blue Mountains but reported that they were "stopped by a mountainous country" — like many others after them would be.

Below: **The Hawkesbury River, near Wisemans Ferry, painted by Conrad Martens.**

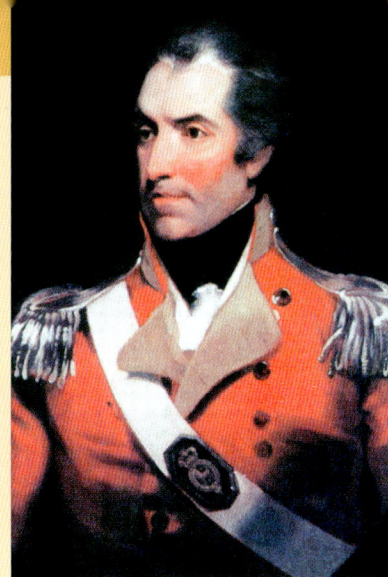

the FACTS!

DAWES, Tench and Captain Hill attempted to tackle the mountains around Parramatta in 1790 but made little progress through the deep gorges of the Wollondilly and Warragamba Rivers.

IN 1793, Captain William Paterson of the New South Wales Corps was the next to try to breach the mountainous perimeter, sending boats up the Hawkesbury, then up the Grose River to the west. Their passage was interrupted by the many cascades and they quit the task, with Paterson writing that they were, "*leaving the western mountains to be the object of discovery at some future day*".

HENRY HACKING was the next to try in 1794, but after traversing approximately 35 km of rugged ridges, he admitted defeat in the face of "impassable barriers".

WHEN THE SYDNEY colony was first established, some of the cattle escaped and vanished. Henry Hacking later found a herd of around 60 cattle at a place now called Cowpastures, near Camden.

PORT HACKING was named after Henry Hacking, who was later transported to Van Diemen's Land for stealing!

Above: Bruny d'Entrecasteaux (1739–93).

the FACTS!

THE SOURCE OF THE rumours of Frenchmen on the Admiralty Islands was reportedly Governor John Hunter, who, after the wreck of the *Sirius*, had returned to England. On the way, he told French captains in Batavia that he had seen Aborigines wearing the red and blue colours of France's naval livery.

Above: Many Australian places, including Point D'Entrecasteaux and Bruny Island, are named after this explorer or his ships.

D'ENTRECASTEAUX came within 70 km of La Pérouse's wrecked ships when he sailed into the Santa Cruz Islands. He even saw the island, Vanikoro, on which two survivors may still have been alive and named it Isle de la Recherche — the Island of Discovery — ironically, he failed to explore it.

JUST BEFORE HE WENT to the guillotine in 1793, King Louis XVI is said to have asked, "Is there any news of La Pérouse?"

BRUNY d'ENTRECASTEAUX died of scurvy on the voyage home. When his crew made it to Surabaya in 1793, they were to learn that the revolution had claimed their king and that France was again at war.

IN 1827, Irishman Peter Dillon traced the wrecks to Vanikoro after finding the hilt of a French naval officer's silver sword.

Further afield
— visits from the French

While the settlers at Sydney were rapidly discovering New South Wales on foot, the French were organising another naval expedition to Van Diemen's Land, determined to follow up the earlier disappearance of La Pérouse.

WITH THE DISAPPEARANCE of La Pérouse's expensive expedition and the chance to found a French colony in New Holland still viable, the French sent Bruny d'Entrecasteaux to carry out investigations of Van Diemen's Land in the *Recherche* and the *Esperance,* and to find La Pérouse.

Charles Stanley's 1849 watercolour painting of the D'Entrecasteaux Channel, Tasmania.

1791, HIS INSTRUCTING OFFICER, Comte de Fleurieu (France's minister of the marine), ordered him to explore Australia's southern coastlines not yet claimed by the British, before sailing on to New Caledonia, the Solomons, New Guinea and then around the northern and western coastlines of Australia.

D'Entrecasteaux ignored these orders. He had heard rumours of French survivors on the Admiralty Islands, so instead he sailed there after re-provisioning at Van Diemen's Land. D'Entrecasteaux had no way of knowing this would lead him further away from the actual wreck site of La Pérouse's ships — Vanikoro in the Santa Cruz Islands. However, d'Entrecasteaux's explorations in 1792 were not in vain. He discovered the D'Entrecasteaux Channel, which was described as "situated at the ends of the world, and so perfectly enclosed that one can consider oneself separated from the rest of the universe", and extensively explored the Derwent River. All the while, his expert hydrographer, Beautemps-Beaupré made excellent maps of the Tasmanian coast, which were later seized by the British.

ON THE WESTERN COAST, D'Entrecasteaux sailed past King George Sound, discovered by George Vancouver in 1791, and south as far as Esperance Bay and the Recherche Archipelago. He continued along the Great Australian Bight to chart territory last explored by Dutch navigator Peter Nuyts in 1627.

Below: The serene waters of Tasmania's Recherche Bay, named after one of d'Entrecasteaux's ships.

The odd couple
— Bass & Flinders

Brave friends George Bass and Matthew Flinders sailed the tiny 2.5 m Tom Thumb *around the shores of Sydney Harbour and south as far as the Georges River in 1795. In 1796, in a slightly larger vessel,* Tom Thumb II, *they explored even further.*

BASS AND FLINDERS were just 23 and 21 years of age respectively when they made one of the most daring explorations of the coastline. The two met on the deck of the HMS *Reliance* as it sailed to Sydney Cove and bonded over a shared love of navigation. Bass had brought with him a tiny row boat, the *Tom Thumb*, which, fitted with a mast and sails, would bear the two men as far south as the Georges River. Governor Hunter was pleased with their work. In 1796 he gave the men a larger boat, a 4.5 m vessel named *Tom Thumb II*. The boat was still cramped, but in it Bass and Flinders discovered Port Hacking and sailed as far south as Lake Illawarra.

Above: In 1797, with Flinders away in South Africa, Bass and six oarsmen rowed a whaleboat south to find the Shoalhaven River, Wilsons Promontory, Western Port Bay and Bass Strait, which bears his name.

Above: Matthew Flinders (1774–1814)

Above: Sydney Cove today.

the FACTS!

BASS was a rather solid man and almost 2 m tall, while Flinders, at 1.6 m tall, was much shorter and slighter. The disparity gave them a rather mismatched appearance when together.

THE *TOM THUMB II* sheltered from a terrible gale in Providential Cove, which is now better known as Wattamolla in Sydney's Royal National Park.

Above: Wattamolla, where the *Tom Thumb II* took shelter, is now a popular picnic site.

BASS returned from his journey to Western Port reporting that a strait was likely to be nearby because of the strong swell he had experienced on his trip to Western Port; however, he had not sailed into Bass Strait to prove this beyond a doubt. To do so, in October 1798, with a crew of eight, Bass and Flinders sailed together again — this time in the sloop *Norfolk,* which had been built of Norfolk Pine.

IN THE *NORFOLK,* Flinders and Bass circumnavigated Tasmania, proving, in Flinders' words, *"that a very wide strait did really exist between Van Diemen's Land and New South Wales, and also now that we had certainly passed it"*.

THREE MEN IN A TUB

On their second journey, Bass and Flinders set out in the *Tom Thumb II* and took with them ship's boy, William Martin, and enough bread, meat and watermelons to last them ten days. Within two days, large waves had capsized the boat, but the men persevered. They replenished their water supplies at Lake Illawarra and sailed on; however, running low of provisions, they were forced to turn back on the fifth day, making it only as far as Bass Point, near Shellharbour.

That night the tiny boat was tossed on dangerous seas in a fierce squall. "A moment's inattention could have sent us to the bottom," Flinders wrote. At daybreak, they took shelter from the fierce seas in a small cove, which they named Providential Cove.

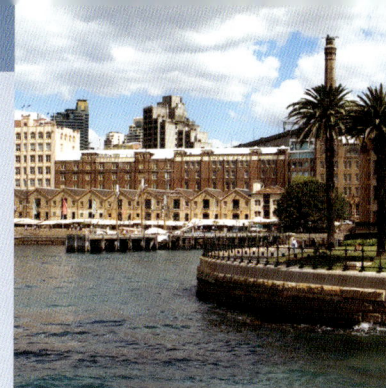

Above: For the duration of the storm, Bass held the sail firm while Flinders steered and the cabin boy, William Martin, bailed water out frantically.

Above: Nicolas Baudin (1754–1803).

the FACTS!

FRENCHMAN François de Saint-Allouarn had sailed to the west coast and claimed an island near Shark Bay for Louis XVI in 1772. However, the French did not settle.

BAUDIN WAS CONSIDERED a harsh captain and his crew appeared to have little faith in his navigational abilities. However, his journal was never published so much of what is written about him comes from Péron, who may have given an unflattering account of Baudin's personality and abilities.

THE FRENCH CREW devoted time to studying the Tasmanian Aborigines, and their body of anthropological observations gives some of the best information about these tribes, as seen in the illustration below.

BOUGAINVILLE'S SON, Hyacinthe, served as a midshipman on Baudin's voyage. Baudin did not consider him a useful crew member.

THE HOSPITALITY the Sydney colony offered the French was not repaid. Soon after Baudin's death at sea, François Péron wrote to the governor of French-owned Mauritius about the settlement, "*It should be destroyed as soon as possible. Today we could destroy it easily; we shall not be able to do it in 25 years time … By means of it, England founds an Empire*".

Charting
the coastline

The discovery of a strait dividing the mainland from Van Diemen's Land was of great interest to the French. If it were true, then the fertile land d'Entrecasteaux had described would not be part of New South Wales, leaving it up for grabs.

Two eager expeditions sought to capitalise on the discovery of Bass Strait, and both French and English expeditions were hastily commissioned.

NAPOLEON BONAPARTE had recently come to power in France and was keen to establish a reputation for himself as something other than a would-be dictator. He dispatched Captain Nicolas Baudin, with a large group of scientists and savants, to discover possible French territory in present-day South Australia and Tasmania in the ships *Le Naturaliste* and *Le Géographe*. He was also instructed to search for the much hypothesised (but as we now know, non-existent) strait dividing the middle of the continent.

Above: Baudin's ships *Le Géographe* and *Le Naturaliste*. The ships sailed much of the expedition apart, with Captain Hamelin at the helm of *Le Naturaliste*.

IN ENGLAND, Captain Matthew Flinders at just 26 years of age, was making ready to further explore the land south of the strait named after his good friend. The two captains were later to meet twice, once on the coast of South Australia at Encounter Bay and again when Baudin, his crew weak with scurvy and malnourishment, recuperated at Port Jackson in June 1802.

BAUDIN'S EXPEDITION was plagued with misfortune, his two boats were separated, his hydrographer accidentally drifted off in a longboat, his crew suffered scurvy, and Captain Flinders had already charted much of the territory they intended to "discover". However, Baudin and his crew did manage to chart Maria Island and further survey the Derwent River and the east coast of Tasmania.

BY THE TIME THE FRENCH ships arrived at Port Jackson, the crew was short-staffed (due to the many deaths on board), weary and ill. Governor Phillip Gidley King, who had taken up command of the colony, treated the French very well, despite Britain and France being at war. The men recuperated at Port Jackson for five months, during which Flinders shared with them his maps of the coastline, a decision that was to cost him much in the future.

Above: Plaque on Middle Percy Island, Qld.

Above: George Baxter's painting of the *Investigator* rounding Cape Wilberforce, Northern Territory, was based on a similar work by William Westall, the landscape artist on board Flinder's ship in 1802.

Around the island
— Matthew Flinders

Flinders, at just 26 years of age, was a gifted navigator. On his return to England after his voyages with Bass, he persuaded Banks to support him in making a complete survey of the coasts of New Holland and New South Wales.

EVEN BY THE END of the 18th century the Australian coastline remained only partly mapped. Western Australia was still referred to as New Holland, and the east coast known as New South Wales. Many still believed the continent to be two islands divided by a channel from the south's unexplored area to the northern coast of Arnhem Land. Flinders was to solve the question of whether Australia was one island or many.

JOSEPH BANKS enthusiastically supported the idea of Flinders charting the entire continent and the HMS *Investigator* was equipped and ready to sail by 18 July 1801. On his voyage, Flinders at first charted much of the South Australian and Victorian coastline before sailing into Sydney on 9 May 1802. He then re-navigated the east coast, taking with him the smaller *Lady Nelson* (in which John Murray and Charles Grimes had discovered Port Phillip Bay in 1802) as a scout ship, and adding detail to Cook's earlier maps.

BY THE TIME they reached the Torres Strait, the *Investigator* was taking on water. Flinders sailed into the Gulf of Carpentaria and put to rest the idea of a channel separating the inland. In November, faced with the onset of the monsoon and a ship fast becoming unseaworthy, he sailed to Timor for repairs before charting a course down the west coast, making only brief investigations before returning to Port Jackson in June 1803. By this time, the *Investigator* was rotten through. Flinders, in command of the *Porpoise*, sailed for England to request another vessel to complete his survey. Flinders' luck appeared to be fast running out. The *Porpoise* struck a reef (now Wreck Reef) and Flinders and his crew of castaways were forced to cover 1100 km of ocean in the ship's two cutters to reach Port Jackson — a feat achieved in just 13 days. Later, after picking up the survivors of the wrecked *Porpoise*, he set out for England in the *Cumberland*. En route he was imprisoned in Mauritius and his aspirations of further voyages went unfulfilled.

the FACTS!

JUST THREE MONTHS before he set sail, Matthew Flinders married. He intended to take his wife with him, but when Earl St Vincent chanced upon Ann Flinders on board the *Investigator* (without permission to be there) and sitting on her husband's knee "without her bonnet on" (apparently a shocking breach of etiquette), Flinders was not allowed to take her. As a result, he didn't see his wife for 13 years!

IN OCTOBER 1802, the *Investigator* sailed carefully through the waters of the Great Barrier Reef (above). Flinders' admiration of this natural wonder was reflected in his journal entry. He wrote that it was *"… glowing under water with vivid tints of every shade between green, purple, brown and white; equalling in beauty and excelling in grandeur"* even the most vibrant of flowers.

IN DECEMBER 1803, Governor de Caen of Mauritius detained Flinders for more than six years, during which time the French beat Flinders to the punch, publishing maps in 1807 that show Gulf Bonaparte instead of Spencer Gulf and Gulf Josephine where Flinders had named Gulf St Vincent.

FLINDERS' book *A Voyage to Terra Australis* was published the day before he died and placed in his hands on his death bed. He was unconscious, so never knew that his work had come to fruition.

Above: Convicts sometimes envied Aborigines.

the FACTS!

MARY BRYANT was transported to Botany Bay for stealing a cloak. Soon after her arrival on 18 March 1791, she and her husband, William, her three-year-old daughter and her one-year-old son, along with a small gang of other escapees, stole the governor's personal cutter and rowed it to Timor. The voyage took ten weeks. When they arrived they were arrested and sent back to England to be tried. Mary's husband and children died on the trip, but she was pardoned and became known forever after as "the girl from Botany Bay".

LT. JOHN SHORTLAND made the discovery of coal at present-day Newcastle while he was chasing on-the-run convicts who had stolen the schooner *Cumberland* in 1797.

WHEN OXLEY ARRIVED IN Moreton Bay, he found three missing convicts who had been living with Aborigines for seven months.

OF ALL THE CONVICT adventurers, the most famous is "Wild" William Buckley (below). Surveyor John Wedge found Buckley, dressed only in animal skins, near Geelong in 1835. Buckley was an escaped convict who spent 32 years living with Aborigines — he had even forgotten how to speak English. The government pardoned him and he went on to work as an Aboriginal interpreter.

Against all odds
— remarkable journeys

Unhappy tales of lives lost are matched by some seemingly miraculous escapes. Many of Australia's pluckiest explorers were escaped prisoners. With little but a convict shirt on their backs, they made some incredible voyages.

WHEN GEORGE BASS was making his amazing journey of discovery in a whaleboat, he came across survivors of the shipwrecked *Sydney Cove* making an even more incredible journey of survival! The three footsore, starving men (fourteen others had perished on the journey) had struggled hundreds of kilometres through dense scrub from Cape Everard to Port Hacking. It took them six weeks and they lived only on what food they could forage along the way. The route that they travelled is today well worn and better known as the Princes Highway. Francisco Pelsaert's journey from the Houtman Abrolhos Islands to save the traumatised survivors of the *Batavia* wreck, and Flinders' trip from the wreck of the *Porpoise* to Port Jackson, are similarly remarkable journeys of human endurance.

BULLY BLIGH'S "SCARCE CREDIBLE" JOURNEY

William Bligh was not a popular man. Although he rose to the ranks of governor of New South Wales (before being arrested and deposed), his nickname was "Bully Bligh" and his path to Government House was paved with hardship. Bligh's brief stint as governor is often overshadowed by his journey as the overthrown captain of the HMS *Bounty*. Bligh and eighteen others were cast adrift in a longboat on 28 April 1789, when Fletcher Christian and his band of mutineers seized the *Bounty* near Tahiti, where the attentions of the local women were reciprocated. Several men and their Tahitian women later retired to Pitcairn Island, living there undetected for almost two decades. With just a dim memory of Cook's navigational maps, a cupful of water a day, small rations of bread and the occasional raw "body, entrails, beak and feet" of sea birds, Bligh steered the survivors to Restoration Island, where they gorged themselves on oysters. Living on shellfood, turtles, dogfish, birds and the raw flesh of a dolphin, the men survived a remarkable voyage of more than 6000 km to reach Timor and safety. Bligh remarked, "Our bodies were nothing but skin and bones, our limbs were full of sores, and we were clothed in rags".

Below: Artist Robert Cleveley depicts Bligh and his men attempting to land at Tofoa, where one man was killed by the hostile local inhabitants.

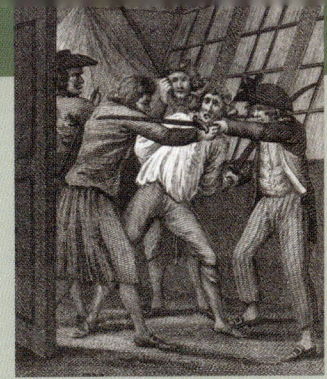

Dead or alive?
— unlucky sea voyages

Daring and death-defying they may have been, but life at sea was risky and many explorers never made it home. Some faced wreck and ruin on deserted islands, others succumbed to disease and yet others ran foul of the "natives".

The life of an explorer was an exciting one, but rarely a long one. Few of the men whose names grace the pages of our history books went on to live happily ever after.

CAPTAIN COOK'S first and second journeys made him famous around the globe; however, his third voyage was to be the death of him. Cook was speared by formerly friendly natives in Kealakekua Bay, Hawaii, on 14 February 1779 after an argument over a stolen boat. On hearing of his death, King George III is said to have wept. Of all the fatalities that could befall one at sea, shipwrecks accounted for many deaths all around Australia's rugged 36,000 km coastline. *Batavia*, *Tryal*, *Zeewyk*, *Zuytdorp*, *Sirius*, *Sydney Cove*, *Pandora* and *Porpoise* are just some of the names that make up a catalogue of early Australian maritime disasters.

OTHERS, such as the *Ridderschap van Holland*, were thought to have suffered the same fate but were never recovered.

the FACTS!

A SAILOR NAMED Forby Sutherland has the dubious honour of being the first confirmed European to be buried on the east coast of New Holland. He died a few days after the *Endeavour* landed and was buried near Botany Bay.

NICOLAS BAUDIN had tuberculosis and died before his voyage was completed.

BY THE TIME the *Endeavour* returned to England, only 56 of the original crew of 94 men remained alive; this was a fairly good rate of survival among sailors at the time!

GEORGE BASS left Port Jackson aboard the *Venus* in February 1803, and subsequently vanished. Some reports suggested he may have been captured by the Spanish and forced to work in silver mines in Lima, but they were unsubstantiated and there is no way of knowing the truth of the matter.

THE PROMISING young seaman John Thistle, on Flinders' crew, was killed when the cutter in which they had been searching for fresh water was battered against rocks and sank, claiming all souls on board.

Above: The HMS *Pandora*, wrecked in the Torres Strait, 1791.

Below: Francesco Bartolozzi based this painting on Cook's "assassination".

BLIGH'S REVENGE

The crew of the HMS *Pandora* successfully located and captured the *Bounty* mutineers, incarcerating them in a small cell on deck known jokingly as "Pandora's Box". With the prisoners on board, the ship ran aground on a reef in uncharted waters of the Torres Strait on 28 August 1791. Thirty-five people died. Ironically, those who survived, which included some of the mutineers, then had to face much the same fate as Captain Bligh — starvation and thirst until they were rescued. Bligh must have thought it fitting justice, indeed. Rescue did the mutineers little good — the three surviving mutineers were hanged all the same when they reached England.

Above: Pack horses were valuable animals.

Exploring the
wide brown land

the FACTS!

THERE WAS MUCH theorising on what might be found in Australia's inland. Some convicts even believed that they would make it to China by escaping and trekking north!

BY FAR THE MOST COMMON assumption was that Australia's centre must conceal a vast inland sea. The explorers who had this idea were more than a few millennia too late. Australia did have a huge inland sea, but only during the Cretaceous period some 65 million years ago!

AUSTRALIA'S desolate interior (above) was to prove a heart-breaking — and often life-taking — disappointment for many explorers. Where they envisioned the glittering waters of an inland sea or a large lake, they discovered only the country's most formidable deserts extending for thousands of kilometres.

EXPLORATION BY SEA was still being undertaken, with purpose-built sliding-keel vessels such as James Grant and John Murray's *Lady Nelson* venturing into Victorian waters. On land, free settlers and convicts would both aid with exploration — pushing further and further out from the colony in the effort of making roads, felling timber and settling land.

Further navigators would go on to explore the country's coasts and rivers, but the focus of 1800s exploration was the search for wealth over land. Explorers sought fertile plains, rivers, timber, mineral resources and the ever-elusive inland sea.

Exploring the continent over land presented new and different advantages and disadvantages to those experienced by sea captains voyaging over the sea.

ONE ADVANTAGE of land exploration was that explorers and naturalists were better able to find, catch, track and record fauna. They were also able to make more detailed observations of the areas they passed through than those made from a ship at some distance from the shore. A major disadvantage was that they were more exposed, subject to the mercy of the elements and the moods of Australia's Aboriginal peoples. A lack of water, rugged terrain, dense scrub and warlike natives would thwart many attempts.

THE FIRST PROBLEM with overland exploration from the colony at Sydney Cove was the rugged ring of mountains that encircled the colony. The Blue Mountains would prove a challenge that few could resist. Much surveying work of the hinterland had begun. John Shortland had made the fortuitous discovery of coal near the Hunter River, which was followed by Bass and Flinders' discovery of coal on the Illawarra Plain. John Wilson and Henry Hacking had ventured into the New South Wales southern highlands and made favourable reports of "a beautiful country".

WHILE FLINDERS was circumnavigating the coast, James Grant, John Murray and Charles Grimes explored the Victorian coastline and discovered Port Phillip. All that was left was for the colony to seek wealth (perhaps the "uncommonly large profit" the Dutch had earlier imagined) in the vast tracts of undiscovered land that lay in the continent's mysterious interior.

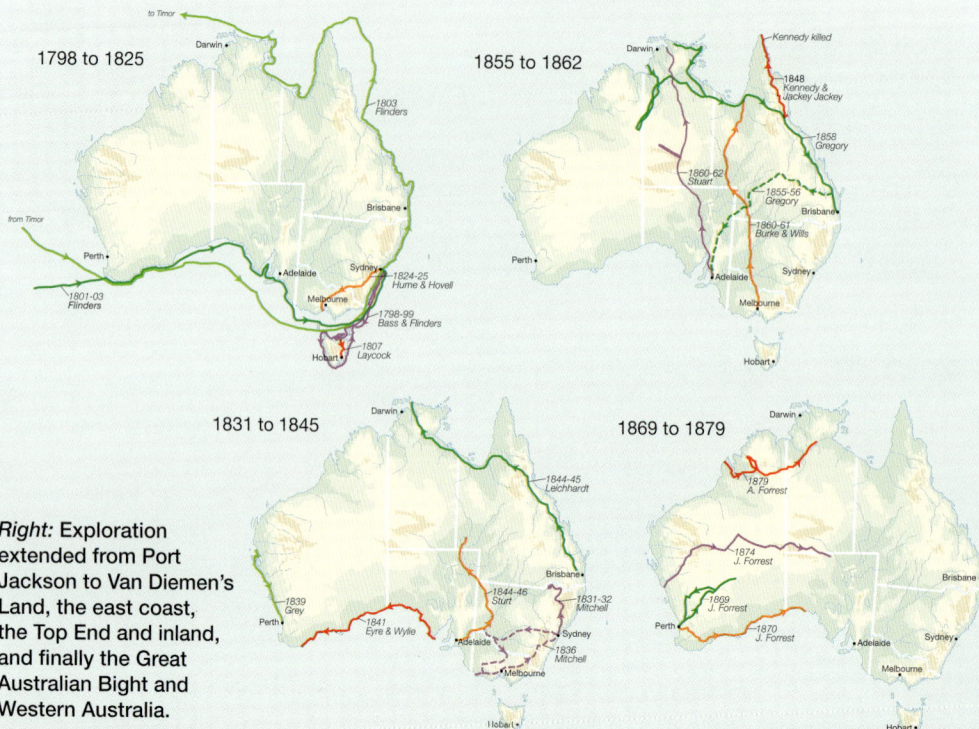

Right: Exploration extended from Port Jackson to Van Diemen's Land, the east coast, the Top End and inland, and finally the Great Australian Bight and Western Australia.

Through the forests

Travelling through the forests was slow going; however, unlike the deserts, at least it provided shade, shelter and firewood.

AS MEN ADVANCED FURTHER into the belt of fertile land along Australia's east and south coasts, the continent — by most former reports devoid of civilisation, wealth or purpose but for the exile of English undesirables — was beginning to be revealed as a place of promise. Australia's inland and hinterland would, in time, yield the mineral wealth that encouraged the gold rushes of future decades. Pockets of forest filled with exploitable timber would be discovered, starting a lucrative timber industry. Rivers, although as variable as the seasons and alternating from a trickle to a flood, would irrigate farmlands to sustain crops and agriculture. Sheep and wheat, especially, would flourish in the new country with profitable results.

AT THE TIME, all of these prosperous secrets lay in wait, over the treacherous mountain pass or outwards from the small coastal settlements that were beginning to be proposed from Van Diemen's Land to Port Phillip. The men who would discover them were the indefatigable overland adventurers.

Above: River systems, if found, would provide water and irrigation for farmlands.

Above: Pasture for cattle and sheep grazing was eagerly sought.

Above: Strong, suitable timber was necessary to establish new settlements.

Above: The gold rush days are recreated at historic Sovereign Hill, Victoria, where visitors can pan for gold.

Above: The Jenolan Caves.

Crossing the
Blue Mountains

Although certainly not high by European standards, the thickly forested chasms and sheer cliffs of the Blue Mountains would prove stumbling blocks for many voyagers attempting to traverse the "Devil's Wilderness" that surrounded the colony.

the FACTS!

THE BLUE MOUNTAINS were formed around 100 million years ago when the sandstone ranges, which used to be underwater, were thrust upward by geological forces.

BARRALLIER WAS THE FIRST European to have evidence of the Koala's existence. He managed to obtain the feet of a Koala (he thought them to be from a monkey) from Aborigines, who had presumably eaten the rest of the animal's body. Barrallier preserved the feet in rum and sent them to the governor.

SNAKES SUPPLEMENTED the diet of the men in Barrallier's expedition party, but he described them as "repugnant to eat".

AFTER BARRALLIER'S failed crossing attempt, Governor King prematurely wrote, "The result of his journey is that this formidable barrier is impassable for man".

OPTIMISTIC CALEY wrote to his patron Joseph Banks, *"though these hills by being seen a long way off, and by the accounts of the few that have visited them, are in general considered as impassable, yet I cannot rank them as such"*.

CALEY AND HIS PARTY quenched their thirst by chewing fruit from native current bushes, which added to their diet of cakes of just-add-water "soup" and salt pork.

CALEY LATER WROTE of the ordeal, *"Sweat poured down in torrents and our clothes were commonly as wet as if they had been dipped in water"*.

DAWES AND TENCH had first tried to approach the mountains from Parramatta in 1790, followed by equally unsuccessful attempts by William Paterson and Henry Hacking. Even the celebrated Bass had set off for fifteen days of "unparalleled fatigue and danger", and although sensibly equipped with ropes, hooks and scaling irons to conquer the mountainous pass he would later be defeated by Hacking's "impassable chasms".

UNDAUNTED by earlier failures, cocky 29-year-old Francis Louis Barrallier, refugee of the French Revolution, would be next to try his hand in 1802. He made preliminary excursions and established huts on a ridge above the Nattai River, where he stored extra supplies. Barrallier made good headway, but was eventually stalled approximately 25 km south of the Jenolan Caves. There, facing hunger, exhaustion and "immense overhanging rocks, which seemed to be attached to nothing, offering an appalling scene", his courage faltered and he retreated to Sydney.

ONE OF BANKS' botanist proteges, the eccentric and confident George Caley, refused to believe that the mountains were impenetrable, at least not for (in his words) "an intelligent and frugal person, provided the weather happens favourable". Caley pushed on from Kurrajong Heights to Govett's Leap, on the way describing the landscape he faced as the "Devil's Wilderness".

FOOD AND WATER ran very low and, unfortunately for Caley, he turned back less than 10 km from Mount Victoria, from where he would have been the first European to see the agricultural promise of the Bathurst Plains. That honour would now be left to three enterprising explorers who cut a route across the ridges — Blaxland, Lawson and Wentworth.

Below: Pulpit Rock in Blue Mountains National Park, with sandstone cliffs beyond. The treacherous country, comprised of deep gorges towered over by crumbling, steep sandstone cliff faces, was to challenge all who attempted to pass through it until 1813.

Ancient landmarks

The Three Sisters at Katoomba are now one of Australia's most visited tourist attractions. Aboriginal legend has it that they are three sisters turned to stone.

THE THREE MOUNTAINEERS

The task that Governor Phillip Gidley King had deemed impossible was finally completed by William Lawson, Gregory Blaxland and William Wentworth in 1813. All of the men were landholders and knew how important it was to find more suitable grazing land for the colony. Blaxland, a family friend of Joseph Banks, left his wealthy family in Kent to take up a grant of approximatley 2000 ha near Sydney. Wentworth, the youngest of the three friends at just 23 years of age, farmed 700 ha near the Nepean River; Lawson, who was a trained surveyor, owned 400 ha near the present-day town of Prospect.

RATHER THAN stumbling through dense forest in the valleys only to run into sheer cliffs, the three friends were keen to attempt a different approach — sticking to the ridge tops. As luck would have it, they started their journey on the main ridge of the Blue Mountains, finding, by fortune alone, one of the only passes that would afford them a crossing. The three friends and an entourage of four convicts and four packhorses set off on 11 May 1813, cutting a swathe through kilometres of "thick brush-wood". Along the way, they backtracked when they came to rocky precipices. Survival also meant clambering down steep hills to the Grose River to refill their water canteens.

BY 25 MAY the small party reached today's Katoomba and by 28 May, from the top of Mount York, the salvation of "forest land, covered with good grass" stretched before them. By the start of June, after climbing Mount Blaxland, the extent of their good fortune was revealed. They compared the luxuriant grasslands of the Bathurst Plain to the biblical promised land of Canaan. Blaxland excitedly wrote that this area contained enough grass to feed all the colony's cattle for 30 years. Although the three explorers had not yet crossed the main range of the Blue Mountains, they were jubilant at their find and returned to Sydney to experience instant celebrity.

Above: Charles William Wentworth (1790–1872) was a headstrong, intelligent man. He went on to become a politician who fought for self-government of the colonies and trial by jury.

Above: Gregory Blaxland (1778–1853) took up viticulture and had a successful vineyard, but was troubled by bowel complaints and depression throughout his later life.

Above: After the Blue Mountains expedition, William Lawson (1774–1850) was rewarded with 1000 ha of land, making him one of Australia's largest landowners at the time.

the FACTS!

WILLIAM WENTWORTH studied law in England and then founded *The Australian* newspaper with his friend Robert Wardell. The paper refused censorship and championed freedom of speech and of the press.

WENTWORTH FALLS (below), in Blue Mountains National Park, is named after the explorer.

WILLIAM LAWSON made three voyages of discovery from 1821 to 1822. During this time he gave the Goulburn River its name and explored around Mudgee.

BLAXLAND'S NAME has gone down in history, but even fame cannot guarantee happiness. Blaxland took his own life on 31 December 1852 after long suffering from depression.

DEVASTATING NEWS came to Wentworth later in life that his father had been sent to New South Wales as a convict and had been charged twice with highway robbery.

Above: The rough road made pastures accessible.

the FACTS!

EVANS WAS no stranger to exploration, he had previously found the Warragamba River in 1804 and crossed a route from Jervis Bay to today's Wollongong in 1812. Evans also had surveying experience, having taken on the role of the acting surveyor-general in Charles Grime's absence in 1803.

IN RECOGNITION of services to the colony. George Evans was given £130 and granted land in Tasmania as a reward for his survey work in the Blue Mountains.

IN 1822 Evans wrote a book about Tasmania entitled *A Geographical, Historical and Topographical Description of Van Diemen's Land.*

COX AND HIS MEN would have had to struggle through the thick forests of the Blue Mountains (below), hacking it away with tomahawks, saws and pickaxes.

IN 1825, GEORGE EVANS was embroiled in accusations that he had received bribes in his work as surveyor-general. The allegations were never fully substantiated and Evans, although dismissed, still received a government pension.

A passage to
greener pastures

The discovery of a pass through the mountains to verdant grassland beyond thrilled the governor, graziers and settlers of the colony. First, however, they had to be able to access the promised land over the mountains.

Blaxland, Lawson and Wentworth had routinely dug "small trenches" to enable their horses to be led down to the river, but the plan to build a road was indeed ambitious.

GOVERNOR LACHLAN MACQUARIE, a man of principle and enterprise, had taken control of the colony after the turmoil of Bligh's deposition. He commissioned George Evans to plan a road over the mountains. On 18 November 1813, Evans departed, at first following Blaxland, Lawson and Wentworth's route over the mountains. Oddly enough, he didn't make distance measurements as he travelled (preferring to make them on his return) but he did make excellent time. It took just one week for him to reach Mount Blaxland, which he named.

EVANS' INSTRUCTIONS had been to extend his exploration beyond the territory covered by Blaxland's party if possible, so he pushed onwards, crossing the main range and finding Fish River in early December. By 6 December, he reached prime grazing country near where the city of Bathurst stands today and named it Macquarie Plains ("the handsomest country I ever saw", he called it) and forded the Macquarie River by building a bridge of felled trees. On his return voyage, Evans diligently measured the distance using surveying-chain measures. Somewhat optimistically, on his return to Sydney he suggested to Governor Macquarie that twelve men "might clear a good road in three months for a cart to travel over the mountains". It took 50-year-old William Cox and a team of 30 well-built convicts twice that time to carve a primitive road 161 km through the rugged terrain to Bathurst.

Above: Governor Lachlan Macquarie (1762–1824) gave a full pardon to the convicts who helped Cox build the road through the Blue Mountains.

Above: George Evans (1780–1852) pushed into the Blue Mountains and found the site of Bathurst.

Retracing rivers
— John Oxley's explorations

Discovery of new rivers north of the Blue Mountains — each confounding in its path and some appearing to flow inland — revived talk of an inland sea.

Evans had great success in his voyage over the Blue Mountains and his subsequent 1815 expedition around Cowra, on which he discovered the Abercrombie, Belubula and upper Lachlan Rivers. Despite this, the stuffy British Secretary for the Colonies (after whom the town of Bathurst is named) decided Evans "does not appear from the style of his journal to be qualified by his education for the task of giving information respecting this new country". Evans was demoted to second-in-charge of a new expedition under Macquarie's new surveyor-general, 32-year-old John Oxley (left).

OXLEY WAS AN EXTREMELY competent surveyor, but he seemed continually disappointed by the land he discovered on his first expedition. On 24 March 1817, Oxley was entrusted with the task of following the course of the upper section of the Lachlan River, which Evans had discovered in 1815. Sensibly, as their task was to explore rivers, Oxley's packhorses carried small boats with which some of the party travelled the river while others traversed the banks. For nineteen weeks Oxley and his men travelled more than 1110 km through what would later prove some of western New South Wales' most lucrative wool-producing regions. On the way, he would discover the Bogan River, Little River and Bell River within days of each other, but he remained dissatisfied. The Lachlan petered out into marshes and the hoped-for inland sea was not found.

IN 1818, Oxley set out from Bathurst in the hope that following the Macquarie River would prove more satisfying. This second expedition proved much more successful. Passing the sites of Dubbo, Narromine and Warren they found the "stupendous" Warrumbungle Range and went on to discover the Castlereagh River, Narrabri and the Nandewar Range; however, the true find was the "hills, dales, and plains of the richest description" that made up the Liverpool Plains. The site where Tamworth now stands and the Peel River also met with Oxley's approval and he felt that "no place in the world can afford more advantages to the industrious settler". On 11 September 1818, the cascades of the Apsley River stalled the party briefly, but they marched on, reaching the ocean on 23 September. By 18 October, the men discovered and named Port Macquarie. Oxley was happy with his discoveries, as this would, "throw open the whole interior to the Macquarie River, for the benefit of British settlers".

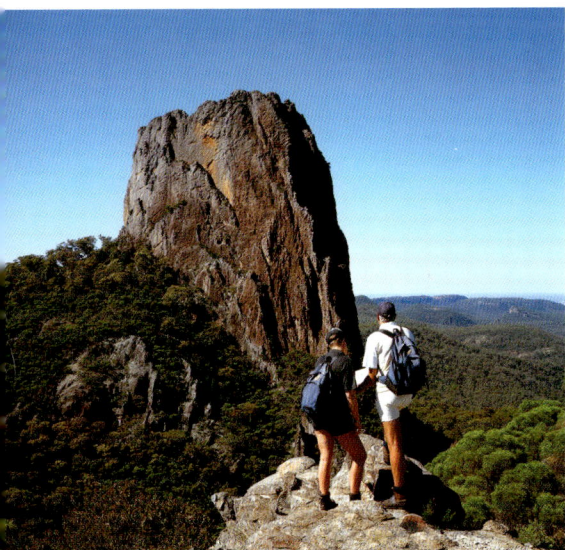

Above: Oxley discovered the Warrumbungle Range, which he called Arbuthnot's Range.

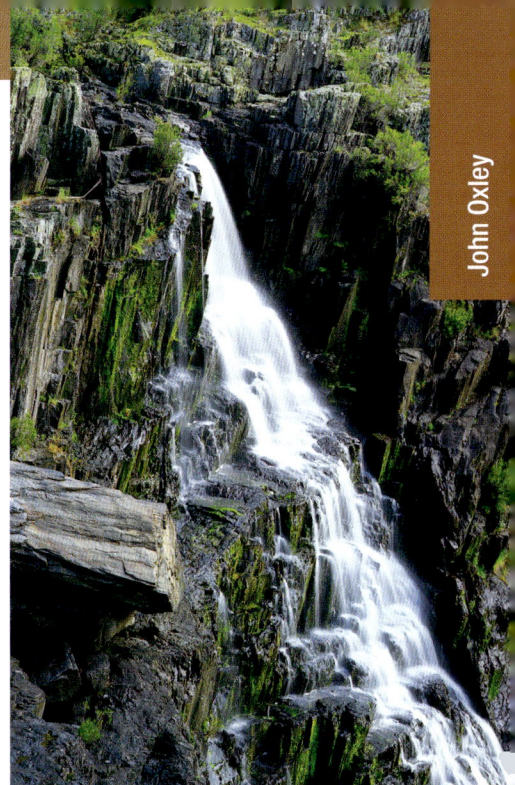

the FACTS!

JOHN OXLEY WAS VERY IMPRESSED with Apsley Falls (above) in the Oxley Wild Rivers National Park, writing, "*We were lost in astonishment at the site of this wonderful natural sublimity, which is perhaps scarcely to be exceeded in any part of the Eastern World*".

GOVERNOR MACQUARIE was disappointed with Earl Bathurst's decision over George Evans, and convinced him it would be "an Act of Justice" to allow Evans to stay on the expedition as second-in-command.

OXLEY KNEW HE WAS indebted to Evans, who accompanied him on his expeditions in 1817 and 1818. He wrote, "*The obligations I am under to Mr Evans for his able advice and cordial co-operation throughout the expedition, and, as far his previous researches had extended the accuracy and fidelity of his narrative was fully exemplified*".

LATER IN HIS CAREER Oxley went on to chart the course of the Hastings River, find the site of Brisbane and chart Queensland's Moreton Bay.

DESPITE FINDING that the Lachlan and the Murray ended in marshes, Oxley didn't give up his idea that the inland sea must exist.

Above: Leichhardt is thought to have owned this travelling clock.

Life for an
overland adventurer

Flies, filth, hunger, thirst, battling through thick scrub or stumbling across drought-stricken aridlands — such were the challenges faced by inland explorers. The best of them were fit, resilient bushmen who knew when to rely on Aboriginal aid.

the FACTS!

EVERY DAY, explorers had to load up the packhorses by hooking on to the saddle heavy saddlebags containing provisions and equipment.

SEEDS FROM NARDOO plants were ground up into a flour and baked into loaves. They filled hungry bellies but had little nutritional value.

CAMELS were not used until 1846, when John Horrocks had the idea of importing dromedaries for expeditions in the arid interior. Unfortunately, his infamous camel, named Harry, was an extremely cantankerous beast. It bit both the goats and the men in the expedition party, bolted with its load and eventually bumped Horrocks when he was unloading his gun, causing its master serious injury. Horrocks later died from his wounds.

WARBURTON WROTE, *"No Australian bushman even thinks himself badly off if he has a quart pot, a blanket for himself, a pair of hobbles for his horse, and a little flour, tea, sugar and tobacco for provisions".*

ON LONG VOYAGES explorers often had the responsibility of droving sheep, cattle or goats, which would make up part of their food rations later in the journey.

Whether driven by curiosity, a sense of duty, a love of adventure or the desire for riches or fame, Australia's explorers had one thing in common — courage.

LIFE IN AUSTRALIA'S untamed wilderness was unpredictable and difficult, made doubly so by the threat of thirst, starvation and attack from Aborigines. Explorers often journeyed into the traditional lands of several groups of Indigenous people on each expedition, mostly uninvited and often unwelcome. The men usually left obvious tracks of their passing and travelled slowly, so were afforded little protection in the event of a concerted attack. Poor weather or injuries could further hinder progress. If a packhorse or bullock used for pulling the dray was injured or died, the expedition could be forced to go slower still and face great peril. Even after an exhausting or catastrophic day, many explorers carefully recorded the day's travels in their journals, describing the disappointments and delights that served to make their voyages so gruelling and yet so interesting.

Above: At night, in a "bivouac" around a campfire, explorers must have felt vulnerable.

PACK LIGHTLY BUT WELL

Knowing what to pack, and how much of it, was incredibly important. The essentials — meat (often salt pork), tea, sugar, flour (for damper), soap, rum and water — had to be taken. Bullocks or horses towed drays or wooden carts (below) stocked with provisions covered with tarpaulins.

MEDICAL SUPPLIES were basic and many illnesses were not well understood. Opium and carpenter's chalk were used to treat diarrhoea, lime juice was taken to prevent scurvy, and Chlorodyne (made up of morphia, chloroform, Indian Hemp and prussic acid) was used to treat serious illness by knocking the injured man out cold.

Tools of the trade

Compasses and telescopes were necessary instruments, but even more helpful was the theodolite, which allowed bearings on both a vertical and horizontal plane.

MAKNG ACCURATE MEASUREMENTS

A critical task for explorers travelling overland was recording the distance and direction travelled. First, they needed to be able to find their own way home and, second, they had to be able to direct others how to find what they had discovered.

EQUIPMENT USED TO SURVEY

on land was similar to that used by the early navigators. Many of the explorers had naval or marine backgrounds, so they knew how to work the instruments used on ships. Compasses were essential for direction, although magnetic iron ore in the landscape sometimes played havoc with them. The direction of the sun or moon and their height from the horizon could also be used, as could constellations, such as the Southern Cross, at night.

TO MEASURE ALTITUDE, explorers

used an instrument known as an artificial horizon, which was like a little spirit level filled with mercury. Altitude could also be figured out by measuring at what temperature water boiled in a billy. Water boils faster at high altitudes.

ONE METHOD OF RECORDING

DISTANCE was to have someone (often a convict) push a perambulator — a wooden wheel that recorded the revolutions at each stage. Obviously, perambulators were not much use over rugged territory, where Gunter Chains were often used instead. These chains comprised 100 metal links, each of about 2 m long, allowing surveyors to measure up to around the length of a cricket pitch.

WATKIN TENCH'S JOURNAL

gives a good description of how he measured distance. He used the compass for direction and counted paces (2200 of which were said to be a mile) as well as keeping records of landmarks. When they camped at night, he and Dawes used a "traverse table", similar to ones used on ships, to plot their course and figure out how far they were from their setting-off point. This, Tench wrote, was "*an unspeakable advantage in a new country, where one hill, and one tree, is so like another that fatal wanderings would ensue without it*".

DYING FOR A DRINK

Keeping, carrying or finding enough water to survive was a constant problem. After icy Antarctica, Australia is the driest continent on Earth — a fact that was to be the bane of many explorers. Barrels of water were taken and refilled as sources of fresh water were discovered on the journey. Each explorer also carried a flask with a rationed amount in it. Sometimes, wells were dug to find water or Aborigines were forced to lead the explorers to soaks in the ground. Explorers also learned that hunger and thirst could be alleviated by chewing the leaves of some native plants, such as the narcotic Pituri plant and the Nardoo, an aquatic fern.

Right: Charles Sturt's watter bottle. Sturt also made large water containers out of bullock skin.

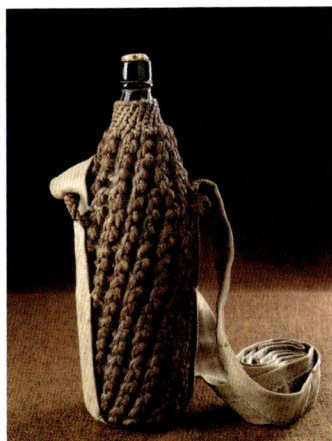

the FACTS!

A CIRCUMFERENTOR was a simple version of the much more effective theodolite. Circumferentors were made up of a brass plate that had bearings for 360° of the compass etched on it. It was set up on a hill, matched to the compass point and bearings were recorded.

THEODOLITES were comprised of a telescope mounted in such a way as to be able to move in both a vertical and horizontal plane, allowing bearings to be taken both astronomically and geographically.

IN 1817, Oxley was upset to find that the mercury had leaked out of his artificial horizon, which was "shaken by the horse forcing his way though the scrub".

WHEN RATIONS RAN LOW explorers often had to eat their bullocks, horses or camels. Sometimes the animals were so scrawny that they provided very little meat. Warburton said, *"We were compelled, by absolute starvation, to eat our last camel all but the hair — clean through from end to end".*

EXTREME HEAT began to dry out the waterhole near Sturt's camp at Depot Glen, so he decided to make waterbags of bullock skins. Almost 950 L could be stored in each bullock skin. The process was as follows. *"A bullock was shot and drawn up by its neck, and carefully skinned from the neck downward, the skin being drawn back over the carcass, leaving the hairy side inwards. It is lashed in a dray, the water poured into the neck, and the huge bottle filled when safe. The orifice was carefully sewed up. In drawing off the water, a string is unfastened at the tail which acts as a spout."*

Above: Phillip Parker King (1791–1856).

the FACTS!

ON BOARD THE *MERMAID* with King were explorers Allan Cunningham, John Septimus Roe and Flinders' trusted Aboriginal guide, Bungaree.

JOHN OXLEY joined King's expedition on the *Mermaid* in 1819 and the two men sailed to Port Macquarie and explored the Hastings River.

THE *MERMAID* had so many rats that they ate into the ship's stores — even chewing into barrels filled with musket ball cartridges!

PHILLIP PARKER KING was awed by the animals he discovered on his trip, writing, "No country has proved richer than Australia in every branch of natural history".

THE HYDROGRAPHIC MAPS King made on his journey were to be used for more than 100 years.

THE *MERMAID* RAN AGROUND near the eastern tip of Cape York. The crew managed to free the cutter and King named the place Escape River. King wrote that, if they hadn't been able to free the vessel, "*there would not have been the least vestige of her the following morning*".

THE FRENCH made another brief visit in 1818, when Louis Claude de Freycinet cruised from the Pacific to South America on a three year voyage. He was sent to follow up on Nicolas Baudin's scientific mission, and returned to France with a huge catalogue of illustrations, notes and natural history observations.

Flinders' protege
— Phillip Parker King

The quickest way to travel long distances was still by ship. With settlements on Norfolk Island and in Van Diemen's Land doing well, the British Government was eager to explore other possible sites for settlement and enlisted Phillip Parker King for the task.

Norfolk-born Phillip Parker King had exploration in his blood. His father, Phillip Gidley King had founded the settlement on Norfolk Island and was later the governor of New South Wales. In his childhood, King was introduced to Matthew Flinders, who made a big impression on the curious young boy.

TRAINED AT Portsmouth Naval Academy, and with marine surveying skills learned from the Admiralty hydrographer himself, Phillip Parker King was an obvious choice for an expedition to explore the parts of the coast not already charted by Flinders. The desired outcome was the discovery of a waterway that would "lead to an interior navigation" — the mythical inland sea again.

TO ACHIEVE HIS AIMS, King took the cutter *Mermaid* with nineteen men and sailed out of Sydney on 22 December 1817. Sailing south to Twofold Bay, King George Sound and North West Cape, they found little but desert. Here, King, blasted by the dry, hot winds coming from the inland, became sceptical of the inland sea theory. Sailing north, they passed through Macquarie Strait and in mid-April discovered and named Port Essington, which King was sure would one day be "a place of great trade".

ON 21 MAY, King sailed through Apsley Strait before returning to Sydney via Timor (to resupply) and Tasmania. On his journey's next leg in the refitted *Mermaid* he sailed first to Port Macquarie and then up the east coast to the Endeavour River, on the way adding detail to charts of the Great Barrier Reef. After charting much of the Gulf of Carpentaria coast, he sailed for Timor, then back to Sydney. Later, in the *Bathurst* (the *Mermaid* having succumbed to rot), King surveyed Rottnest Island and north to the earlier-discovered North West Cape. On completion of his four-year sojourn, King had mapped nearly 1100 km of the east coast and nearly 1200 km of the north-west coast, as well as some of the South Australian coast.

Above: The *Mermaid* was only just saved after running aground on Cape York Peninsula.

Below: Scrubby, dry Port Essington proved to be an unsuitable site for a settlement and was quickly abandoned.

Historic highways
— opening up the interior

Above: Charles Throsby (1777–1828).

Scattered pockets of grazing land were being reported around the region that is now New South Wales, as well as areas to the south and north. The challenge now was to link up these areas by land.

Many of the routes trodden by Australia's explorers in an effort to connect rivers, lakes and plains to settlements, later became the roads that would make travelling across this vast continent possible.

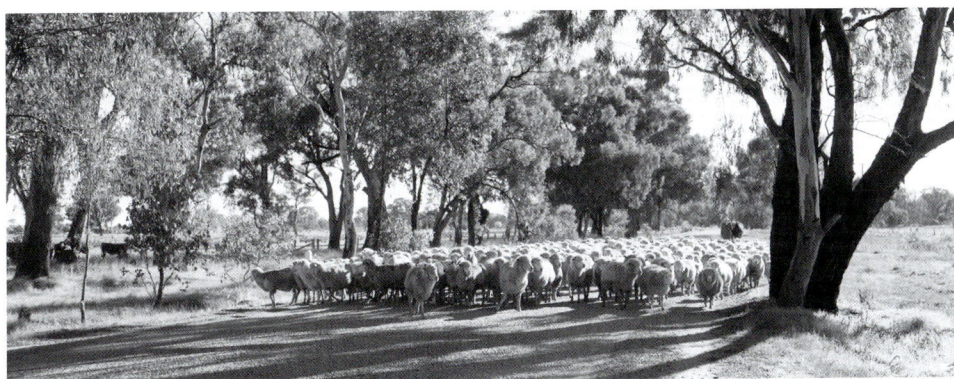
After early agricultural development, the Hume Highway, Victoria, became a vital link between the coast and tablelands. Its present route follows in the footsteps of pioneers such as Hamilton Hume.

CONVICTS PLAYED AN IMPORTANT role in building and shaping the face of Australia, particularly in exploration. In 1818, Macquarie sent emancipated convict turned deputy surveyor-general, James Meehan, to find an overland path from the Sutton Forest to Jervis Bay. Hamilton Hume and Charles Throsby were among the expedition party. On the journey, the party split into two, with Meehan's group going on to discover Lake Bathurst and the Goulburn Plains.

CHARLES THROSBY, commanding the other group, crossed the Shoalhaven River to the north of where the town of Nowra now stands and made it to Jervis Bay, the planned destination, on 3 April 1818. Hume was later to become a renowned explorer, spending the following four years trekking through land west of Goulburn, discovering the Yass River and Plains in 1822. The Hume Highway today traces his wanderings. Meehan was far from the only ex-convict to enjoy success at exploration. Ex-convict Joseph Wild had discovered Lake George in 1820 and the Murrumbidgee (with Charles Throsby) in 1821. In 1823, he accompanied Brigade-Major John Ovens and Commander Mark Currie in their quest to find pastures to the south of the lake, along the way charting the path where the Monaro Highway now runs today.

Below: The Monaro Highway was built once settlers flocked to Monaro Downs near Cooma.

the FACTS!

CHARLES THROSBY (above) believed that white settlers and Aborigines could live in peace and that killing Aborigines to "teach them a lesson" only prompted revenge attacks.

THE WORD YASS is taken from *yarrh* — an Indigenous word that means "running water".

THE MONARO DOWNS were at first named Brisbane Downs after Governor Sir Thomas Brisbane (below), who replaced Macquarie in 1821. The governor went on to lend his name to Queensland's capital.

ILLITERATE CONVICT
Joseph Wild was sentenced to transportation in 1793. He went on to make quite a name for himself. He received a conditional pardon and accompanied Barrallier, Throsby, Meehan, Ovens and Currie on expeditions. Later in his life, he was even made a constable!

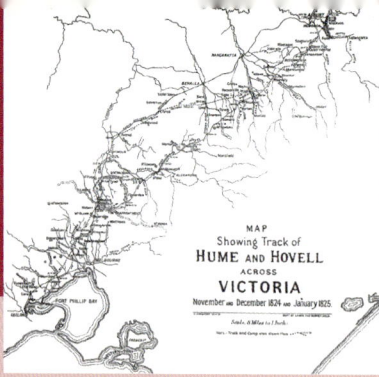

MAP
Showing Track of
HUME AND HOVELL
ACROSS
VICTORIA
November and December 1824 and January 1825.

Above: Hume and Hovell's route.

the FACTS!

HUME WAS BORN in the colony, so was taunted as a "currency lad" by the other "sterling" (English-born) settlers. However, his familiarity with the Australian environment would later be to his advantage. He began exploring the bush around his home at Appin when he was just 17, taking with him his 14-year-old brother and an Aboriginal guide.

HOVELL AND HUME took with them 91 kg of salt pork, 290 kg of flour, 6 kg of tea, 45 kg of sugar, 4 kg of tobacco and 5 kg of soap. However, by the time they reached Broken River they were surviving on flour, water and game they shot.

HUME WAS A CAPABLE bushman, hunting kangaroos and Emu, catching fish and constructing makeshift rafts to cross rivers. In one instance, the explorers made mocassins out of bullock hide to cover their bare, blistered feet.

THE MEASUREMENTS MADE on the journey became even more incorrect when the explorers' perambulator fell apart during the voyage.

ABORIGINES who Hume and Hovell encountered near Port Phillip Bay wanted them to come and meet William Buckley, the escaped convict who had been living with them for years. Hume declined their offer.

HUME AND HOVELL fought quite a lot on the journey, at one time even breaking the only frying pan by arguing over who should take it should they part ways. After their expedition they quarrelled even more! Public bickering over who had led the party, caused a rift between the two men that was never mended.

Hovell & Hume
— grand discoveries

Sir Thomas Brisbane replaced Governor Lachlan Macquarie in 1821 and was instructed to keep the settlement of new regions tightly controlled. "Not a cow calves in the colony but her owner applies for an additional grant," he complained.

With the governor seemingly uninterested in exploring further pastures, landowner William Hovell — who had himself discovered the Burragorang Valley in 1823 — teamed up with seasoned explorer Hamilton Hume and the two men struck out to make explorations of their own beyond the Murrumbidgee River.

THEIR EXPEDITION across Victoria was one of the most ambitious and successful, but for a few critical errors. Taking six convicts, six horses and two bullock drays, Hovell and Hume set out from Appin on 2 October 1824, travelling through Mittagong and Goulburn then arriving at Hume's property in Gunning. Hovell, who was keeping navigational records, was already worried that his instruments were not trustworthy and was calculating the party's position by dead reckoning along with an odometer and perambulator.

ON THE JOURNEY, Hume and Hovell crossed the Murrumbidgee, spotted the Snowy Mountains, discovered the mighty River Murray (which they named Hume River), Mount Buffalo, the Goulburn River and Mount Disappointment and ended their journey at Corio Bay, near Geelong, which Hovell mistakenly believed to be Western Port due to his imprecise

measurements. This error almost discredited the men when a settlement was later established at unsuitable Western Port, rather than the actual site of Corio Bay, which the men had described so favourably. Hume and Hovell subsequently argued over who had led the party, and whose fault this was, for years.

Above: Hovell and Hume's party crossing the Murray River in 1825, having made a raft out of boughs and a tarpaulin.

Below: On 8 November, 1824, "a prospect came in View the most Magnificent, this was an immense highe [sic] Mountain Covered nearly one fourth of the way down with Snow and the Sun shining upon it gave it a most brilliant appearance". Hume and Hovell were awed, of course, by the sweeping vista of the Australian Alps. Oil painting by George Peacock.

North to
New England

Australia was fast becoming a land of opportunity for all. Remarkably, even a sick, shy botanist from Kew Gardens was able to make a name for himself by discovering some of Australia's most significant agricultural land.

Allan Cunningham was quite unlike most of Australia's other explorers. He arrived in Sydney Cove in 1816 as a botanic collector for England's Kew Gardens and was given permission to join John Oxley and Phillip Parker King's sea voyages, on which he made many observations and collected specimens. These voyages must have instilled in the quiet naturalist a passion for discovery.

IN 1822, GOVERNOR BRISBANE

agreed to Cunningham's suggestion of an expedition to find a passage for stock from Bathurst to the Liverpool Plains. Frail and suffering from tuberculosis, Cunningham seemed an unlikely man to complete the task successfully — in fact, he almost failed in his quest on a number of occasions, but although weak in body, his strength of character prevailed.

ON 15 APRIL 1823, taking a party of five servants, five horses and ten weeks worth of food, he embarked on his mission. The terrain was steep and rugged — a place of "frightful irregularity", he noted — and his men and horses struggled to find a pass through the many ravines. By May, the exhausted party returned to Cassilis by way of the present-day sites of Scone and Merriwa. Cunningham, however, was determined to find a way through. In a final, desperate attempt to breach the mountainous pass, he chanced upon the point where the Warrumbungle Range meets the Liverpool Range, and a passage through the mountains was found. Cunningham named it Pandora's Pass. Within the year, scores of graziers drove their cattle through the passage to settle the rich farmlands of Australia's New England region.

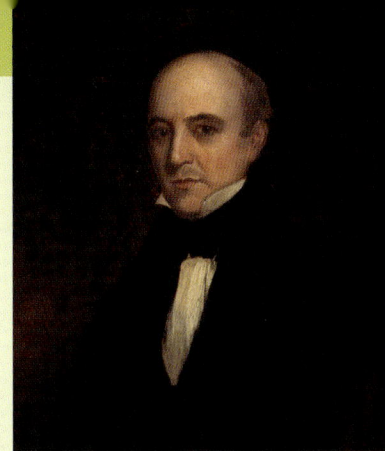

Below: Once Allan Cunningham opened up Pandora's Pass, graziers drove cattle from stations near Scone and Merriwa (below) north to pastures in the New England region near Tamworth.

Above: Allan Cunningham (1791–1839).

the FACTS!

BEFORE he became a botanist, Allan Cunningham (above) studied jurisprudence in England.

ON CUNNINGHAM'S FIRST expedition attempt, he was forced to walk more than 200 km back to Bathurst in humiliation after losing his packhorses.

PANDORA'S PASS WAS NAMED after the Greek myth about Pandora, the woman who released the emotion "hope" to the world. Cunningham named it so because it was pure hope that made him make his final, successful attempt to cross the mountains.

THE PARTY buried a memorandum under a marked tree in the pass. It was marked 9 June 1823 and read, "*Buried for the information of the first farmer who may venture to advance so far to the northwards of this vale, of whom it is requested this document may not be destroyed, but carried to the settlement of Bathurst, after opening the bottle*".

THE MEMORANDUM also said that the explorers had planted some peach pits in Pandora's Pass "*with every good hope that their produce will one day or other afford some refreshment to the weary farmer*".

CUNNINGHAM RECEIVED no reward for his discovery of the Darling Downs, although the servants he took with him each received £10.

Above: Major Edmund Lockyer
(1784–1860).

the FACTS!

IN 1825, Major Edmund Lockyer had explored the Brisbane River, which had been discovered by Oxley in 1823. Lockyer found good soil and coal, as well as the Stanley and Lockyer Rivers.

THE GAP THAT CUNNINGHAM noticed from Warwick was not the one that he would eventually pass through on his journey from Moreton Bay. The one he saw was Spicers Gap; the one he passed through was Cunninghams Gap (below).

MORETON BAY was deemed a suitable place for a penal settlement, so Captain Patrick Logan was sent to establish the settlement in 1826.

THE DARLING DOWNS WAS named after Governor Ralph Darling.

OXLEY WROTE of, "*Downs of rich, black and dry soil, and very ample surface; and as they furnish an abundance of grass, and are conveniently watered, yet perfectly beyond the reach of these floods, which take place on the flats in a season of rains, they constitute a valuable and sound sheep pasture*".

Superior country
— the Darling Downs

In 1827, Cunningham made a discovery that far surpasses that of Pandora's Pass. In 1824, he visited Moreton Bay with John Oxley, and conceived the idea of an overland expedition from New England to Moreton Bay. This voyage, in 1827, revealed the Darling Downs.

In a south to north attempt, Cunningham first marched over the inland on 30 April 1827, leaving from Segenhoe, a large property on the Hunter River. The path taken was initially over the Liverpool Range, to the east of the Liverpool Plains, then on to the Peel River and north along the rugged eastern edge of the Nandewar Range.

CUNNINGHAM'S PARTY TRAVELLED relatively smoothly at first. By 25 May they reached the excellent farming land around the Macintyre River. The day after, Cunningham wrote of "a handsome piece of water, evidently very deep", which was named the Dumaresq River. Oxley had unwittingly discovered the two rivers that now make up part of the south-western border between Queensland and New South Wales.

SWINGING NORTH-EAST on 5 June, Cunningham and his team looked upon "a superior country … exceedingly cheering to my people". Although the area was in drought at the time, Cunningham was extremely impressed. He described, "an extraordinary luxuriance of growth". Crossing the Condamine River, they passed by the site of Warwick and noted a spot in the main range that might "prove a practicable pass". However, his men and pack animals were fatigued after their tiring three-month journey and, after discovering the Gwydir River, they returned to Segenhoe station.

CUNNINGHAM'S TASK of discovering a way to connect South-East Queensland's richest agricultural lands to the Moreton Bay penal settlement was successfully completed by approaching Main Range from the opposite direction.

HE SAILED TO MORETON BAY in 1828 with Captain Patrick Logan and trekked south-west, eventually discovering Cunninghams Gap, through which the highway named after this determined explorer now passes.

Below: Today, the Darling Downs offers some of Australia's most valuable agricultural lands for crop production and grazing.

All the rivers run
— Sturt's search

Above: Captain Charles Sturt (1795–1869).

Oxley's earlier work in seeking the source of the Macquarie River was soon superseded by an extensive boat journey undertaken — much to Major Thomas Mitchell's dismay — by 32-year-old British Army captain Charles Sturt.

Above: Sheep graze in fertile green fields on the Murray River floodplains.

Sturt had impeccable credentials, but little practical experience in exploration. However, he led his expedition team on a long and winding route through Australia's complex network of intersecting rivers with integrity and sound judgement.

DROUGHT works a dramatic change on the landscape, so the rivers Sturt passed appeared very different to those Oxley encountered years before. Sturt's descriptions of "emus, with outstretched necks, gasping for breath [searching] the channels of the river for water, in vain", give a good indication of the desolation.

IN 1828, STURT followed the course of the Macquarie River and added another major river (the Darling) to the patchwork of inland waterways. The next year, he followed the Murrumbidgee to its destination at Lake Alexandrina, taking to a whaleboat when reeds blocked the way. Eventually, the whaleboat was swept into a "broad and noble river", which Sturt named the Murray River. Another junction proved a serpentine reach of the Darling.

STURT AND HIS MEN reached Lake Alexandrina in February 1830. They had intended to sail into Gulf St Vincent, where a boat would carry them back to Sydney. Their plan was ruined by the patchwork of ephemeral channels and alluvial sandbanks that hinder Lake Alexandrina's passage to the sea. This unlucky circumstance forced them to turn around and row against the strong current of the Murray River to return to their camp at Narrandera — an incredible journey of more than 3000 km in Sturt's estimation.

STURT RETURNED to Sydney, where his success was front-page news. The *Sydney Gazette* reported "Captain Sturt has inscribed his name in indelible characters upon the records of our history". Sturt's expedition had been a success, although he himself wished that the land he found was more fertile. He was not to know that within years irrigation techniques would transform land into a wealthy food-production area, or that paddlesteamers would soon ply the river he named the Murray.

the FACTS!

HAMILTON HUME, along with two soldiers and eight convicts, accompanied Sturt on the expedition, which also had 15 horses, 10 bullocks and a whaleboat wheeled along on a small cart.

ON THE MURRAY RIVER near Wentworth, the expedition attracted a "vast concourse of natives" and narrowly avoided being attacked. Sturt had made friends with an Aboriginal man earlier in the journey; luckily, his Indigenous friend appeared and convinced the others to let the men pass.

MURRAY COD (right) were plentiful on the river at the time of Sturt's journey. He wrote that the men had eaten so many of these fish that they lost their appetite for them.

STURT also discovered the Bogan River. The name is taken from an Aboriginal word, which means "birthplace of a king".

ON THEIR RETURN JOURNEY Sturt's men existed on a diet of damper and a little salt meat each day. Added to their hunger was their exhaustion — the men formed shifts and rowed from daylight to daybreak with just an hour's break to eat their scant rations!

JUST WHEN it seemed certain that all of them were doomed to starvation, the expedition party caught and ate some swans, which sustained them just enough to make it back to Narrandera.

Above: Sir Thomas Mitchell
(1792–1855).

Australia Felix
— Sir Thomas Mitchell

Few would argue that Sturt's travels had not been a success — apart from the controversial explorer, Thomas Livingstone Mitchell, whose nose was decidedly out of joint about not being chosen for the expedition himself.

"GEOGRAPHICAL RESEARCH cannot be entrusted with advantage to amateur travellers," wrote Mitchell haughtily. Mitchell took over from John Oxley as the surveyor-general of New South Wales in 1828. By all reports, he was a difficult yet thorough man. Soon after taking up his post he started to make a general trignometrical survey of New South Wales, which his predecessor Oxley had maintained was not achievable.

BY 1831, MITCHELL was organising his own expeditions. He firmly believed that rivers would run off the bulk of the Great Dividing Range to form a basin — the discovery of an inland sea was still on his agenda. On 30 November 1831, the expedition departed from the Hunter River, travelling slowly due to the many detailed measurements Mitchell demanded. On this journey, Mitchell found neither a northern river nor the inland sea he hoped for. On 6 February 1832, he headed home, his expedition a failure.

the FACTS!

WHEN GOVERNOR DARLING appointed Thomas Mitchell to the role of surveyor-general he wrote that he "*could not say too much in favour of Major Mitchell's zeal and qualifications*". However, just two years later, Darling had a different opinion of the determined surveyor-general, writing that it was "*impossible to carry on the service with any prospect of advantage or hope of success, should Major Mitchell be continued in the situation of Surveyor-General*".

MITCHELL'S HOPES WERE influenced by lies told by a convicted armed robber, George Clarke. Apparently George possessed knowledge of a large river, which the Aborigines called the Kindur, where he had seen "Hippopotamuses and Ourang Outangs". That Mitchell — by nature a critical thinker — gave any credence to the convict's fabrication is as incredible as the story itself!

MITCHELL INSTRUCTED his team to find out as many Aboriginal place names as possible to be marked on his maps. Thanks to this, a lot of Australian cities and locations retain their traditional Aboriginal name.

IN 1844, after being knighted in England, Sir Thomas Mitchell returned to Australia and entered politics. He became the member for Port Phillip, but soon ran foul of Governor Gipps, who remarked, "*the Member for Port Phillip may act as he please … the Suveyor-General of New South Wales must both obey, and support the government*".

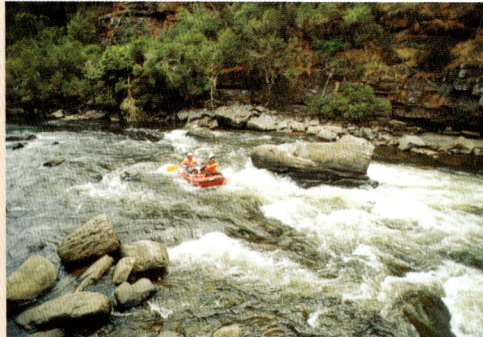

Above: The Mitchell River, named after the explorer, is popular for whitewater rafting.

THREE YEARS LATER Mitchell attempted another expedition. He suspected that the Darling River, discovered by Sturt, would lead northward. On 7 April 1835, Mitchell's well-provisioned band of explorers left Boree Station for the Bogan, arriving at the Darling by 25 May. After travelling almost 500 km, Mitchell had to admit Sturt was correct — the Darling flowed south. In 1836, he set off again, this time with more success. He discovered the Wimmera, Mount Arapiles, the Glenelg and Fitzroy Rivers, Castlemaine, Kyneton, and the Campapse and Coliban Rivers. On his maps, Mitchell marked his finds "Australia Felix" — the most "felicitous" land for settlement.

HIS FINAL EXPEDITION set off in December 1845 and included 80 bullocks, 250 sheep (for food), 17 horses and Edmund Kennedy as his second-in-charge. Mitchell's aim was a route to the Gulf of Carpentaria, and as he believed in a north-flowing river he intended to find that also. On this journey he found the Barcoo River (the headwaters of Cooper Creek). Mitchell also found valuable pastoral land across Central Queensland. Despite his difficult character, Mitchell was an excellent explorer and a highly accomplished man. He was a competent artist and writer, fluent in Portuguese, and even patented a boomerang propeller for steamships later in life.

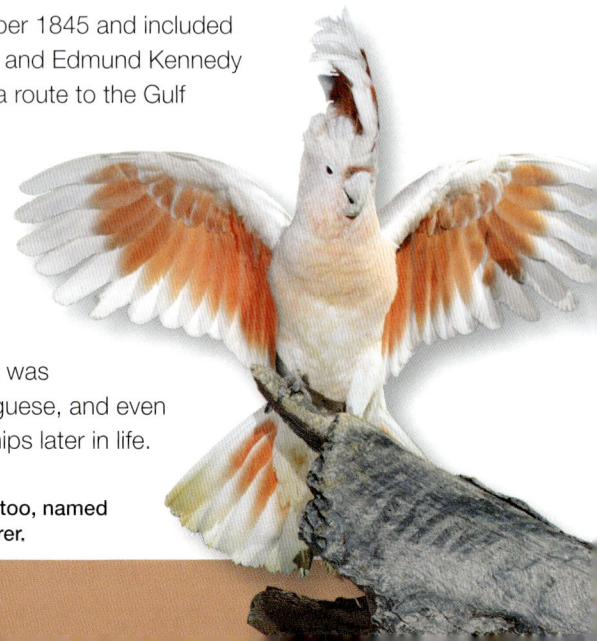

Right: Major Mitchell's Cockatoo, named after the multi-talented explorer.

Creating more colonies

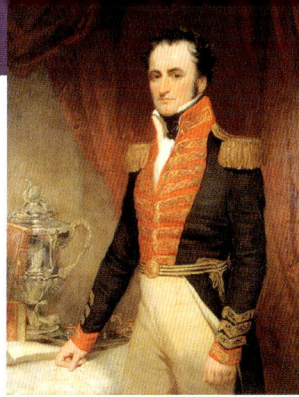

Left: Captain James Stirling (1791–1865).

While settlers were spreading out across the colony of New South Wales, expeditions had taken place to find other likely places for colonies. Men such as Stirling, Stokes, Batman, Logan and Light would foster expansion in the other States.

From as early as 1800, James Grant in the *Lady Nelson* surveyed the Victorian coast, followed by John Murray and Charles Grimes. John Bowen established the settlement at Risdon Cove, Tasmania, in 1803, when the Sydney colonists were struggling to cross the Blue Mountains. In the years to follow, settlements at the present-day sites of Brisbane, Perth, Darwin and Adelaide would be built.

Above: Edwin Augustus Porcher's watercolour of 1845 depicts the isolated settlement of Port Essington in the Northern Territory.

THE WORK OF THOSE WHO founded Australia's State capitals was usually preceded by the efforts of other, often overlooked men. Port Phillip would never have become the site of today's Melbourne were it not for Charles Grimes' survey and discovery of the Yarra in 1803. In a similar vein, the Moreton Bay settlement owed much to Oxley; and William Light's founding the "free settler" city of Adelaide was made possible only by the hard work of Collett Barker in 1831. John Bremer claimed the northern coast for Britain in 1824 — years before John Lort Stokes, sailing the *Beagle* in 1839, was to name Port Darwin, which was later settled as Palmerston by George Goyder in 1869. Much of the Territory's toughest exploration was carried out by John Roe and James Bremer around "the most useless, miserable, ill-managed hole in Her Majesty's dominions" (according to Thomas Huxley) — Port Essington. Edmund Lockyer (fresh from his discoveries in Queensland) and Charles Freemantle were to make similar claims on the Western Australian coast in 1826 and 1829 respectively, and James Stirling's settlement, later Perth, was established the same year.

the FACTS!

CAPTAIN JAMES STIRLING was effusive in his praise for the region around the Swan River in Western Australia, writing, *"I represent it as the Land, which, of all that I have seen in various quarters of the World, possesses the greatest natural attractions"*.

VAN DIEMEN'S LAND WAS the site of much early expansion, with John Bowen, Colonel William Paterson and David Collins all establishing outposts there in the early 1800s.

Above: Sullivans Cove in Tasmania, the site of David Collins' settlement in 1804.

JAMES KELLY sailed around much of Tasmania's west coast in a whaleboat in 1812–16. The missionary George Robinson also travelled around the island on foot.

MELBOURNE was lucky not to be called "Batmania" — the name favoured by one of the settlement's founding fathers, John Batman!

THE MORETON BAY colony was established at Redcliffe before moving to the site of Brisbane.

OF ALL of the settlements that went on to become capitals, only Adelaide and Darwin have unblemished histories. Tasmania, Norfolk Island, Moreton Bay and Perth were founded as convict settlements.

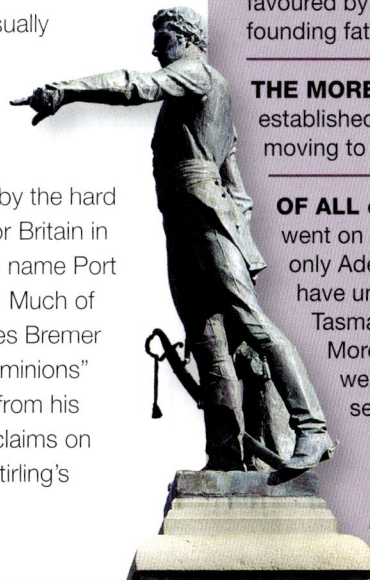

Left: Colonel William Light.

Above: Snowy Mountains.

Into the
snowy country

The discovery of the Australian Alps was truly astonishing in its unexpectedness. That a country so hot and dry in places could contain mountains reminiscent of the European Alps in miniature stunned the explorers who gazed upon them.

the FACTS!

LHOTSKY set off with little food or water and took just one horse towing a cart stocked with needles for pinning insects, paper for preserving specimens, and books.

LATER IN HIS LIFE, Lhotsky took up journalism, interviewing "Wild William Buckley" (who had lived with Aborigines for 32 years) and quizzing him on geographical points of his travels and about the Aboriginal language.

STRZELECKI'S NAVIGATIONAL skills and scientific work were sometimes questionable. His maps were later found to have the courses of rivers wrong. He also made the bizarre suggestion that if an Aboriginal woman mated with a European, she would then be biologically unable to mate with an Aboriginal male. His completely false theory was treated with the derision it deserved by anthropologists and London's *Ethnological Society Journal*.

ANGUS MCMILLAN describes a meeting with an elderly Aboriginal man in the mountains who, having never seen a horse before, shook hands with all of the white men, and then went through the same motions with each of the horses in turn, shaking the bridles "very heartily".

ON HORSEBACK in 1842, William Adams Brodribb expanded upon the routes travelled earlier by McMillan and Strzelecki.

Hovell and Hume were the first to espy the frosted Alps, but the real alpine exploration was left to men better used to snow-covered terrain — Czech Johann Lhotsky, Scots George Mackillop and Angus McMillan, and Polish adventurer Pawel de Strzelecki.

LHOTSKY, A TRAINED BOTANIST and doctor, arrived in Sydney in 1832 with the intention of becoming the colony's zoologist. He was unsuccessful in this, so in 1834, with some government funding, he set out to explore the "very heart of the Australian Alps" instead. Naively believing he would be able to stock up at "inns" along the way, Lhotsky took few provisions. Fortunately, squatters were hospitable and he obtained supplies at Robert Campbell's Limestone Cottage before "hitting the slopes". On 16 February, he reached the site of Cooma and then discovered the Snowy River and today's Thredbo before he noted, "the waterpots were covered with ice an inch thick" and it became "impossible to go farther".

A YEAR LATER, on a more easterly course, George Mackillop was able to cross the Snowy River at Jacob's

Above: Twilight colours the Alps.

Ladder and reach the luxuriant Omeo tableland, where he established the historic 24,300 ha Strathdownie Station. Another callleman with big dreams, Angus McMillan (who was the manager of Currawong Station on the Monaro), began his journey in 1839 marginally better equipped than Lhotsky, taking with him a pocket compass, one of Flinders' old charts and an Aboriginal guide. McMillan found and settled pastoral property at Ensay before setting out in 1840 with a party of six, including two Aborigines. His expedition revealed the sites for Bairnsdale and Bruthen, as well as Lake Victoria and the Nicholson, Mitchell, Perry, Avon, Macalister and Thomson Rivers.

COUNT STRZELECKI was to complete McMillan's mission of finding a route through to the sea in 1840, travelling McMillan's earlier path and forging on to Western Port. He also become the first person to climb Australia's highest peak, Mt Kosciuszko, which he named after the Polish democratic leader. Strzelecki's expedition was an arduous one. His emaciated expedition party only made it to Western Port by surviving on wombats and Koalas, which had been caught by their Aboriginal guide.

Along the Bight
— Edward John Eyre

Above: Edward Eyre (1815–1901) at 29 years of age.

At just 24 years of age, brave young Edward Eyre tempted fate by undertaking a gruelling journey across the Nullarbor Plain. Even Governor Gawler advised against it, but what followed was an epic feat of endurance and determination.

The desperation of Eyre and Wylie's situation, and the friendship between them, is captured in this watercolour by Gordon Woodhouse.

DEPARTING FROM PORT LINCOLN in 1840, Eyre and his party first set up a depot at Streaky Bay before reaching Fowlers Bay on 17 November. Eyre had already lost three horses. Had he pressed northward, as expected, he could easily return to Fowler's Bay (the last viable port for thousands of kilometres) to meet a ship. For reasons unknown, Eyre took four men — his friend John Baxter and three Aboriginal guides and set off with six sheep, eleven horses and a small dray carrying provisions — into the bleak wilderness towards Western Australia.

THE HEAD OF THE BIGHT was reached on 2 March 1841. By 7 March, water was in short supply. Eyre rode ahead to search for water, but the overall journey of many days failed to find any. "We had been four whole days and nights without a drop for our horses," wrote Eyre on 11 March. Only some Aboriginal wells at Eucla were to save them. The party was still about 1000 km from their destination at King George Sound, and had only three sheep, 64 kg of flour, and 500 ml of water (each) per day. The horses were so weak that the men had to walk. Providence came to the rescue again when they caught fish and found water by digging between some sandhills.

BY MID-APRIL, the Eyre party was forced to eat the weakest horse. Calamity struck again on 29 April when Baxter was shot by two of the Aboriginal guides, who later fled, taking the party's guns and provisions. Eyre and his faithful Aboriginal friend, Wylie, struggled on alone, killing and eating another horse and later feasting on kangaroos, fish and crabs. Rescue came in the unlikely form of a French whaling ship on 2 June, when the men received food, water and rest on board the *Mississippi*. The indefatigable Eyre refused to quit. He and Wylie left the ship and suffered a further 480 km of hardship to reach Albany, Western Australia, on 7 July 1841, as heroes.

Left: Sand dunes near Eucla, where the party found Aboriginal wells that sustained them after hundreds of kilometres with little water.

the FACTS!

WYLIE WAS given a medal from the government along with £2 and rations for life.

EYRE'S JOURNAL records the discomfort experienced by the sand and flies. He said of the sand, "*It floated on the surface of the water, penetrated into our clothes, hair, eyes and ears...*" to make matters worse, he adds, "*we were again inflicted with swarms of large house-flies, which bit us dreadfully*".

AFTER EYRE'S FRIEND John Baxter was shot and killed in a scuffle with the two Aboriginal guides, Eyre wrote, "*the frightful, the appalling truth now burst upon me, that I was alone in this desert ... I was left with a single native ... Ages can never efface the horrors of this single night*".

WYLIE FEASTED ONCE THEY reached better country in mid May. Eyre wrote with amazement: "*He commenced by eating a pound and a half of horse-flesh, and a little bread, he then ate the entrails, paunch, liver, lights, tail, and two hind legs of the young kangaroo, next followed a penguin, that he found dead upon the beach, upon this he forced down the whole of the hide of the kangaroo after singeing the hair off, and wound up this meal by swallowing the tough skin of the penguin; he then made a little fire, and laid down to sleep, to dream of the pleasures of eating*".

AT TIMES ON THE JOURNEY "utmost vigilance" was required to stop the very dehydrated horses from drinking seawater.

Above: Ludwig Leichhardt (1813–48).

Lost in the wild
— Ludwig Leichhardt

After Eyre's daring journey, explorers began to treat their expeditions as adventures of the human spirit, often gambling their lives on increasingly unfavourable odds. Leichhardt made many such journeys, but luck didn't always go with him.

In 1842, Eccentric Prussian explorer Friedrich Wilhelm Ludwig Leichhardt, an enthusiastic botanist who had studied medicine in Berlin and London, arrived in Sydney to begin a love affair with the Australian continent that would one day claim his life.

QUEENSLAND, perhaps above all other Australian States, is a place of great contradictions in nature. Golden beaches and lush rainforests give way to the rugged Central Queensland outback and the tropical wilderness of Cape York. Leichhardt was to traverse much of this country for himself — travelling from Newcastle to Moreton Bay in 1843, discovering the Wide Bay region and later making his way through the Gulf of Carpentaria and Arnhem Land in 1844. In 1848, an attempted east–west crossing was to be his downfall.

LEICHHARDT'S LONGEST VOYAGE was made in 1844–5, when he and a team of ten, living off the land and travelling with horses and bullock drays set off to travel from Moreton Bay to the Gulf — a distance of some 5000 km. On the way, the party discovered Expedition Range, Peak Range and the Suttor, Burdekin, Lynd and Mitchell Rivers. When they reached the Gulf of Carpentaria, their original destination, they carried on south-west.

Above: Carnarvon Range's ridges brought to mind castles of Leichhardt's homeland, hence the name Ruined Castle Valley.

"BUSH TUCKER" WAS PLENTIFUL HERE, so they quickly added the Norman, Flinders, Leichhardt, Nicholson and Roper Rivers to the list of waterways they had found. Soon after, Leichhardt was devastated at having to burn most of his prized collection of plant specimens — three of their horses had stumbled into lagoons and drowned and the bullock drays could not carry the extra load. The men journeyed down the South and East Alligator Rivers, passing through today's Kakadu National Park, to reach Port Essington on 17 December 1845. Everyone had long thought them to be dead. Leichhardt's friend Mr Lynd had even written a funeral dirge for him! They arrived in Sydney in March 1846 to much acclaim and Leichhardt wrote to his brother-in-law, "... no king could have been welcomed with greater gladness and deeper interest by a whole people than I was myself".

Left: The vivid Leichhardt's Grasshopper is named after this explorer.

the FACTS!

WHEN LEICHHARDT'S expedition party of ten men set off from the Darling Downs on 1 October 1844, they were all singing a rousing chorus of "God Save the Queen".

WETLAND WATERHOLES and lagoons (below) across the Top End provided plenty of birdlife to go into Leichhardt's stewing pot.

ON 28 JUNE 1845, the men were attacked by Aborigines and John Gilbert died. Two others, each with two spears stuck in them, required emergency surgery with a sharp knife. Incredibly, within two days the brave wounded men carried on!

THE MEN TOOK A BREAK on 24 May 1845 to celebrate Queen Elizabeth's 26th birthday with a cake and the luxury of sugar in their tea.

THE 1844–45 JOURNEY took so much longer than expected that most people believed the explorers were dead. When Leichhardt met a tobacconist he knew in Sydney, the man ran ahead of him shouting, "*This is Leichhardt! the man we buried long ago! ... He's come from Port Essington and he's beaten the bush!*"

LEICHHARDT RECEIVED a Royal Geographical Society gold medal in 1846.

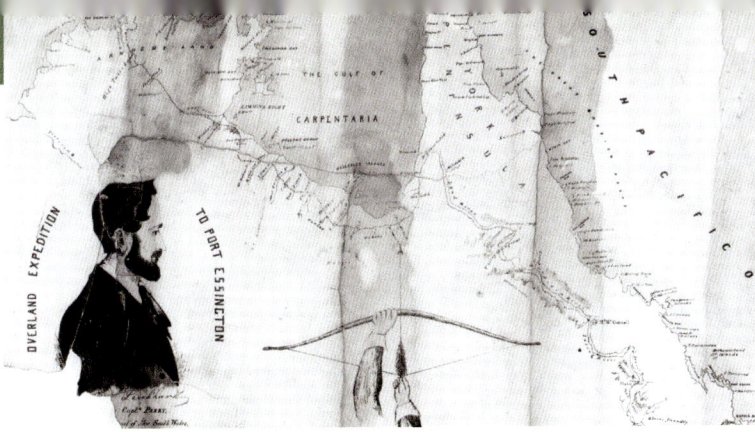

Extensive travels

Leichhardt's navigational skills were later questioned, but he still managed to cover many thousands of kilometres of extremely variable habitat in Queensland and the Gulf of Carpentaria.

DISAPPOINTMENT AND DEATH

Disaster was a companion on Leichhardt's second journey, which departed on 7 December 1846. On this occasion, he and eight other men tried to cross the continent from the Darling Downs to Perth. They were well provided for, with 40 bullocks, 270 Tibetan goats and 108 sheep, as well as horses and mules. The journey took them through, "the most horrible country the foot of a white man ever trod", remarked Henry Turnbull. Wet-season mud and heavy rains destroyed their tents, bogged them down and scattered their livestock. Added to that were paper-wasp attacks, sickness and disease. Leichhardt was criticised for selfishness at this point, but with some recovery time, they pressed on regardless. The horses suffered so badly from flies that their bodies were often, "streaming with blood from the bites". In June 1847, ill with fever and toothache and having achieved little, Leichhardt called the expedition off.

THE EXPEDITION that presumably claimed Leichhardt's life departed from Cogoon Station, near Roma, on 4 April 1848. The men were last seen trekking north-westerly on the banks of the Warrego River before they disappeared without a trace. In 1873, a man named Andrew Hume claimed that a survivor living with Aborigines told him the men had turned on Leichhardt before being killed by Aborigines, but his report was not verified. Numerous search parties were sent out, the latest in 1938, but all proved inconclusive. The truth is out there — somewhere in the Australian wilderness.

the FACTS!

LEICHHARDT and his men wore makeshift ponchos made of calico that had been saturated in oil. This proved very effective against the heavy tropical rain.

HARRY BROWN, one of the Aborigines on the voyage, sometimes sang "corroborri [sic] songs" in his "melodious plaintive voice" to lull the men to sleep.

"WE WERE ELECTRIFIED, our joy knew no limits," wrote Leichhardt on 2 December 1845 when the troupe stumbled upon some Aborigines who greeted them with the words, "'Commmandant!, Come here!, Very good!, What's your name?'"

ON THE SECOND EXPEDITION, flies were in such plague proportions that when the men tried to eat, each spoonful came with the added protein of "about twenty flies"!

SEARCH PARTIES (below) were sent out to discover the cause of Leichhardt's disappearance and recover his body. Henry Turnbull wrote that Leichhardt, "*rests in a holier spot than any consecrated by man ... the sad wind sighs over him, and the warm sun shines on him ... It is just such a resting place as any lover of nature would choose*".

LATER, Frank and Alexander Jardine would travel though similar territory droving cattle from Bowen to the tip of Cape York.

THE NICETIES OF FOOD

To survive, Leichhardt and his men had to eat whenever and whatever they could. By late November 1844, Leichhardt wrote, "It is remarkable how soon man becomes indifferent to the niceties of food." Leichhardt and his men ate goannas, Emus, kangaroos, possums and any birds they could find. A few edible plants, such as wild marjoram, were also on the menu, despite frequently giving the men bowel upsets. Leichhardt sometimes even drank a cupful of Emu oil, which dripped from roasting Emu meat, as "a good anti-rheumatic". When a ripped flour bag spilt 7 kg of precious flour, the men even scraped it up — grit, leaves and all — and made it into a murky mess of porridge, "which every one of us enjoyed highly". Later on the journey, after a meal of pigeon, Leichhardt "swallowed the bones and the feet of the pigeon to allay the cravings of [his] stomach". Flying-foxes also found their way into the party's cooking pot. The men found their flavour a little overpowering, "but in messes made at night, it was always difficult to find out the cause of any particular taste".

Above: Goannas and flying-foxes were stewed and eaten.

Above: Sturt's Desert Pea.

the FACTS!

"LET ANY MAN lay the map of Australia before him, and then let me ask him if it would not be an honourable achievement to be the first to place foot in its centre", Sturt wrote in his journal.

STURT WAS so cheerfully optimistic that he would find an inland sea that he carried a small boat with him and wrote to then Governor George Grey, *"It will be a joyous day for us to launch on an unknown sea, and run away towards the tropics".*

STURT AND HIS MEN were surviving on tea, damper and meat. As a result of this inadequate diet, later in the journey almost all of the men suffered from scurvy, which turned their skin black and made their mouths rot from the inside.

IT GOT SO HOT that the ink for their pens kept drying up, the lead dropped out of their pencils and their hair stopped growing. "Our nails had become as brittle as glass," Sturt marvelled.

TO AVOID THE EXTREME HEAT Sturt and his men dug a deep underground cavern to shelter in, similar to those used by miners in Coober Pedy.

AT ONE POINT on the journey Sturt and John MacDouall Stuart (who accompanied Sturt on the journey) saw a crow dig up some "bacon and suet" that the dogs had buried. "These choice morsels were washed and cooked," wrote Sturt.

Desert Disasters
— Charles Sturt

Eyre's confidence that only sandy deserts lay in northern South Australia was dismissed by his friend Charles Sturt, who maintained belief in the fabled inland sea. There was only one way to settle the argument once and for all ...

Following his Murray River expedition in 1830, Sturt was languishing in the post of registrar-general of South Australia. Despite his health still suffering the ill-effects of his last journey (glare and malnutrition had sent him almost blind), Sturt set out again, at 49 years of age, on what would be his final voyage.

HE DEPARTED ADELAIDE in August 1844 with 15 men, 30 bullocks and 6 drays, 11 horses, 200 sheep, a whaleboat (should he reach the sea!) and permission to venture as far north as 28° latitude. He planned to pass eastwards along the Murray and then venture north along the Darling, thus avoiding the ring of salt lakes that had obstructed Eyre's passage. The party took their time at first, making it to Menindee in two months, where the journey was to become more laborious.

WHEN THEY CAME TO BROKEN HILL and the Barrier Ranges, Sturt sent two men to explore west, but their unfavourable reports of land around Lake Frome and Mount Hopeless led to the party heading north instead. It was a lucky decision — they found water at Flood Creek and later Depot Glen waterhole (near Milparinka), where they established a camp. By now, Sturt was caught in the sweltering heat of the Australian summer. The mercury reached 40°C daily and Sturt, who had been making small excursions into the territory that surrounded them, noted:

> We were then in one of the most gloomy regions that man ever traversed. The stillness of death reigned around us, no living creature was to be heard ... It was marvellous to me that such a country should extend to so great a distance without any change.

For five months, the party were stalled at the depot, waiting for rain before they could even think of continuing the expedition.

Right: Charles Sturt surveys "one of the most gloomy regions that man ever traversed".

Vast nothingness

Sturt and his men were forced to retreat in the face of the unconquerable red sandhills and parching heat of the Simpson Desert.

THE MOST FORBIDDING SCENE

The desert yielded little flora or fauna of any use to the men of Sturt's party. Seeds would not grow and the men began to suffer from scurvy. One man, James Poole, died at Depot Glen from the disease. Finally, rain fell on 12 July 1845 and Sturt sent some of the party back to Adelaide. Had common sense prevailed, the entire party would have returned, but Sturt refused to yield "an inch of the ground I had gained at so much expense and trouble". Another depot, Fort Grey, was set up on Lake Pinaroo at July's end and short expeditions made west and north. Still, Sturt found only arid land.

RATHER THAN RISK THE LIVES of the entire party, Sturt took just three men and enough food for four months and set off north on 14 August 1845, finding Strzelecki Creek and adequate food and water on 18 August. His next find was the bare, silent wasteland of Sturt's Stony Desert on 27 August. Here, his horses had no food but the bark of three sparse trees. Thankfully, by 4 September grass and water were found at Eyre Creek, but to the north-east, water supplies were salt and the men were severely malnourished. "Water and feed had both failed," despaired Sturt, as the party turned away from the Simpson Desert before them to trek back the way they had come.

Above: Endless barren pebbles of Sturt's Stony Desert. *Inset:* Sturt's Desert Rose.

MEANS OF DOING MORE

With his pride at stake, Sturt refused to return to Adelaide "having literally done nothing, and with the means still in my power of doing more". On 9 October, after recuperating somewhat at Strzelecki Creek, the party travelled north to where it meets Cooper Creek and then north-west to Birdsville. The oppressive heat killed two horses and burst their thermometer, yet, when they reached Fort Grey, Sturt was still keen to make one more desperate attempt to reach the inland! His foolhardy suggestion was dismissed by Dr Browne — thankfully for Sturt, who soon collapsed from scurvy and had to return to Blanchetown on a bullock dray. It was, by all accounts, a dismal expedition that only confirmed Eyre's point of view — there was nothing but desert in Australia's inland.

Below: The party established a camp at a waterhole they called Depot Glen, near today's Milparinka. This depot was later to be their salvation.

the FACTS!

THE MEN RODE FROM DAWN to sometimes 6 pm with, *"no shelter of any kind from the tremendous heat of the fiery deserts in which [they] had been wandering, subsisting on an insufficient supply of food, and drinking water that your pigs would have refused"*.

STURT WAS RELUCTANT to quit. He believed that the journey would, *"place his name high up in the roll of fame ... to him who had well nigh reached the topmost step of the ladder, and whose hand had all but grasped the pinnacle, the necessity must be great, and the struggle of feeling severe, that forces him to bear back, and abandon his task,"* he wrote.

AFTER THE EXPEDITION, Sturt arrived at his house in Adelaide at midnight on 19 January 1846. His loving wife Charlotte was surprised and delighted to see him, having believed that he was probably dead.

Above: The Hamersley Ranges were discovered and named by Frank Gregory. Their mineral wealth would later turn men into millionaires.

the FACTS!

BEFORE STARTING HIS MISSION Augustus Gregory sensibly asked the esteemed Sir Thomas Mitchell for advice. True to his grumpy nature, Mitchell refused to help him!

MANY HORSES DIED on the journey. Five were lost just swimming from the ship *Monarch* to the shore at Treachery Bay before the expedition began. Two more died soon after and three were attacked by crocodiles. By 5 January 1856, some of the horses were carrying a load of 82 kg under harsh conditions! A further two steeds died on 23 January by falling into steep ravines. More died from eating poisonous plants. Horseshoes were routinely torn from their hooves. Often, when exhausted, they were killed and eaten. Horses were the silent heroes of expeditions.

ON HEARING THAT mercury in Oxley's "artificial horizon" had spilt on rough journeys, Frank Gregory filled his instrument with treacle.

AUGUSTUS GREGORY first discovered coal in Western Australia in 1846 and in 1848 explored the site of today's Geraldton.

IN 1858, AUGUSTUS GREGORY was sent on a mission searching for Leichhardt in Central Queensland. He and his brother Charles found a tree in western Queensland that was marked with an "L", which he believed was a sign of Leichhardt's expedition, but found no other traces of the explorer.

Pastures & pearls
— the Gregory brothers

In the 1850s, advances in technology and shipping improved communications and transportation, especially for Britain, which now possessed the huge steamship *The Great Eastern* to transport people between continents. The British Government experienced a renewed interest in the unexplored areas of Australia, where mineral wealth and pastoral land might await.

AUGUSTUS GREGORY, a 36-year-old surveyor was granted £5000 pounds in 1855 to conduct a scientific exploration of Australia's north, in search of a new settlement. He and his men trekked an incredible distance from Victoria River to Moreton Bay, following part of Leichhardt's earlier route. Eighteen men accompanied him on the journey, including his younger brother Henry and botanist Ferdinand von Mueller. The party also took 50 horses. At first the men travelled south-west into Western Australia, as far as Lake Gregory, before retracing their tracks and pushing on to Mataranka in the Northern Territory, along the Roper River and across the Gulf to the east coast. The journey revealed excellent pastoral land in the Gulf.

Below: Augustus Gregory (1819–1905).

ANOTHER GREGORY BROTHER, Francis (Frank), was also a successful explorer. He found grazing land around the Murchison River, and then explored the Gascoyne River in 1858, naming Mount Augustus after his brother. In 1861, while looking for suitable cotton-growing areas, Frank found pastoral land around Dampier. One of his most lucrative finds was the pearl beds of Nickol Bay, which he wrote could be of "immediate importance" to the colony. Pearling would go on to become a major industry.

Above: Frank Gregory (1821–88) discovered land that later became an important stock route in Western Australia.

TO COMMEMORATE
THE CENTENARY OF THE LANDING OF
EDMUND B.C. KENNEDY AND PARTY
WHO LANDED TWO MILES SOUTH OF THIS CAIRN
FROM THE BARQUE "TAM O'SHANTER" ON MAY 24TH 1848
TO EXPLORE CAPE YORK PENINSULA.

FAITHFUL ABORIGINAL "JACKEY-JACKEY"
BOTANIST W. CARRON AND W. GODDARD
WERE THE ONLY SURVIVORS
OF THE PARTY OF THIRTEEN MEN.

An untimely death
— Edmund Kennedy

Seeking the destination of the Barcoo River — discovered by Thomas Mitchell — 29-year-old surveyor Edmund Kennedy set off in 1847, returning victorious. The following year, he embarked on a quest to find a suitable port on Cape York Peninsula.

Kennedy's first expedition was successful, although not in the way Thomas Mitchell had hoped. Kennedy, Mitchell's assistant surveyor, had discovered the Thompson River, an important tributary, but his news that the Barcoo joined Cooper Creek discredited Mitchell.

AN EVEN DARKER CLOUD was thrown over Mitchell's discoveries when Governor Charles FitzRoy chose Kennedy to lead an expedition to continue further north of Mitchell's route. Steamers travelling from Singapore to Sydney required a port where they could load coal, so the establishment of a suitable harbour on Cape York was the expedition's aim.

TO AVOID AN UNNECESSARY TREK through already well-explored territory, Kennedy and his expedition party first sailed to Rockingham Bay on the Queensland coast. It proved a difficult landing spot. The surrounding land was mountainous and densely forested. It took the party almost five months to battle through jungle and reach Weymouth Bay. By then, some of the men were sick, so Kennedy left them at Weymouth Bay in November 1848 and carried on with a party of three white men, the Aborigine Jackey Jackey, horses and limited provisions. Kennedy hoped to make up for lost time and reach the ship *Ariel*, which had been instructed to wait for them at Port Albany.

ON REACHING THE Shelburne River, one of the men accidentally shot himself. Leaving the two other men to care for their injured companion, Kennedy and Jackey Jackey travelled on alone. Shortly afterwards, they were surrounded by Aborigines and Kennedy was speared in the back. Jackey Jackey shot at the attacking Aborigines, fending them off for some time while he cut out the barb of the spear that had pierced his friend, but more spears fell and Kennedy met with his untimely death.

Left: Jackey Jackey held off the attack by warlike Aborigines, but it was too late to save Kennedy.

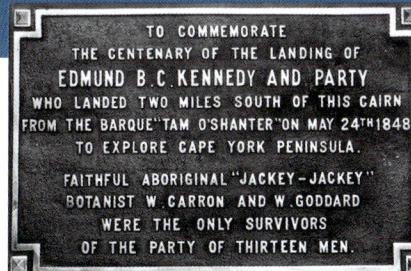

the FACTS!

KENNEDY LEFT for his first expedition on 13 May 1847 and soon disproved Mitchell's theory that the Barcoo ran north to the Gulf of Carpentaria. On this expedition, Aborigines ruined supplies of flour that were buried at the explorers' depot by digging them up and mixing them with clay.

JACKEY JACKEY was just 17 when he was employed as a guide on Kennedy's expedition. His traditional name was Galmarra.

IN A REMARKABLE FEAT of bravery and determination, Jackey Jackey, who had also been wounded above the eye, escaped by wading through water up to his head. He then trekked on alone for a fortnight to reach Port Albany. Amazingly, the ship *Ariel* was still waiting for the men and Jackey Jackey was recognised and able to organise a rescue party to go back for the men at Weymouth Bay.

THE MEN left at Weymouth suffered appalling hunger and illness and died one by one. Botanist William Carron was so emaciated that when he was found by Jackey Jackey and men from the *Ariel* on 30 December 1848 his arm and hip bones were poking through his scrawny flesh. He told of how some Aborigines had given them some victuals, including a Blue-tongue Lizard (right). When it was opened they found it had eleven babies inside. The starving men roasted and ate the lot.

THE THREE MEN left at Shelburne River were never seen again.

CARRON, William Goodard and Jackey Jackey were the expedition's only survivors.

Above: Bungaree

BUNGAREE was the first Aborigine to circumnavigate Australia. He travelled on Flinders' *Investigator* and also on the *Mermaid* with Phillip Parker King.

"I ASKED HIM 'Mr Kennedy, are you going to leave me?' and he said, 'Yes, my boy, I am going to leave you ... you take the books, Jackey, to the captain ...'" Such is Jackey Jackey's poignant report of Kennedy's death (below), after which, Jackey Jackey *"turned around ... and cried. I was crying a good while until I got well"*.

TOMMY WINDICH, on John Forrest's expedition in 1869, routinely led the men to water and hunted game for the party, as well as negotiating safe passage with Aborigines whose lands they passed over. Despite this, he was ridiculed in a formal speech in honour of the expedition for claiming to be, "the man who brought Forrest to Adelaide, and not Mr Forrest him".

WHEN SOUTH AUSTRALIAN Surveyor-General George Goyder went to settle Darwin, he met the Larrakia people who treated him to a corroboree. They sang, in perfect English, "John Brown's Body" and other songs that the Woolna people had passed on to them.

Aboriginal
assistance & friendship

Few of the explorers could have completed the incredible journeys they undertook without the help and friendship of skilled Indigenous guides. These resourceful, resilient Aborigines knew better than anyone the perils of the bush.

Tales of courage, loyalty and perseverance resonate throughout the history of Australian exploration, but few more than those of the Aborigines who accompanied the white men to hell and back on their exhausting journeys.

COURAGE AND KINDNESS shown by many Aboriginal people to those who were effectively invading their native land serve as a reminder that earlier reports of the "hostile brutes" and "savages"— encountered in many studies of Australian history — represent only one side of the story. Jackey Jackey was just one among many Indigenous men and women who generously offered help to the white explorers, often risking their own lives in the process.

BRAVE AND LOYAL FRIENDS

Governor Phillip was the first to enlist the skills of the Indigenous people in an attempt to find food. He considered Arabanoo, Bennelong, Colebe and Yerrawamannie not only honourable, excellent guides, but also friends. Even before the colony was settled, Dampier, Cook and others found the majority of the Aboriginal peoples they encountered were conciliatory, if not friendly.

Above: Wylie was Eyre's faithful friend.

EDWARD EYRE would surely have perished were it not for the unfaltering support of his friend Wylie. Similarly, both Matthew Flinders and Phillip Parker King benefited from Bungaree's level-headed approach to smoothing things over with other Aboriginal tribes. "Guide, companion, counsellor and friend", was how Thomas Mitchell described Yuranigh, of the Wiradjuri people, who guided him through Central Queensland. Leichhardt was astonished at the ease with which his Aboriginal guides navigated and remembered places and landmarks.

ALONG WITH ACTIVELY GUIDING explorers, Aborigines helped in many other ways. "Native-dug" wells quenched many a weary explorer's thirst, as did discoveries of "bush tucker" and traditional methods of catching food, such as the use of weir-like fish traps. Eyre remarked that the Aborigines made him aware of "an almost unlimited catalogue of articles used".

Right: Baudin's artist Petit painted this portrait of Bidgee Bidgee, a "well known native of Sydney who speaks English very well".

South to north
— John McDouall Stuart

Above: John McDouall Stuart said Itirkawara rose up like "a locomotive engine with its funnel".

In 1859, the South Australian Government offered a £2000 reward to anyone who could be the first to cross the continent from the south to the north. John McDouall Stuart, a hardy Scot with a surveying background, jumped at the chance.

Stuart was accustomed to the privations of the life of an explorer. The stoic Scot had travelled on Sturt's inland expedition in 1844, and in 1858 and 1859 he had made minor incursions to the territory around Lake Eyre.

HIS DESIRE TO DISCOVER what lay in the "mysterious interior" was almost an obsession, so the opportunity was simply too good to pass up. On 2 March 1860, the small party set out from Chambers Creek to head north to the Gulf of Carpentaria. Three attempts were required, with the last, in 1862, proving successful when the men reached the Indian Ocean at Chambers Bay. Along the way, Stuart and his men saw and named the Finke River, Chambers Pillar (the pillar of sandstone now known as Itirkawara), the MacDonnell Ranges and Central Mount Stuart — long thought to be the geographical centre of the continent — where they planted the Union Jack in 1860 and left their names in a bottle under a cairn of stones. On the expedition, the men's boots and clothes fell apart and they suffered debilitating scurvy. By 28 October 1862, Stuart was vomiting blood and mucus and could no longer walk or talk. He was "reduced to a perfect skeleton". His men had to devise a stretcher pulled behind two horses to get him home. Stuart died just four years later, his body having never really recovered from the exertions of exploration. The Overland Telegraph Line was later built along his route.

the FACTS!

WHEN STUART'S RIGHT EYE failed, he wrote, *"I now see two suns instead of one, which has led me into an error of a few miles".*

NATIVE CUCUMBER boiled in sugar helped the men recover from scurvy.

AT ONE POINT, Stuart and his Aboriginal guide, on horseback, came across a local Aborigine who had never before seen men on horses. The frightened man climbed up into a Mulga bush. *"What he imagined I was I do not know; but when he turned round and saw me I never beheld a finer picture of astonishment and fear."*

AFTER RAISING THE FLAG on top of central Mount Stuart, the men *"gave three hearty cheers for the flag, the emblem of civil and religious liberty,"* Stuart added ominously, *"... may it be a sign to the natives that the dawn of liberty, civilisation and Christianity is about to break upon them".*

RESOURCEFUL McKINLAY

In 1865, following Stuart's earlier explorations, the South Australian Government sent John McKinlay (who had earlier crossed from Gawler to the Bowen River looking for Burke and Wills) to find a site for settlement in the north. He travelled by sea at first, but by June 1866 was exploring inland. Trapped by floodwaters of the East Alligator River, clever McKinlay constructed a makeshift raft out of the hides of his horses stretched over a timber frame. Amazingly, all fifteen of his party made it across the raging flood after six days of rowing through the crocodile-infested waters. On his return, McKinlay recommended Port Darwin as a suitable colony site. Within four years, George Goyder was sent to found the city that later became Darwin.

Left: McKinlay and his men rowed across the misnamed "Alligator River" in a tiny, flimsy raft made of horse hide.

An ill-fated
expedition

the FACTS!

THOUSANDS OF VICTORIANS farewelled the men from Royal Park when the large expedition party left Melbourne. It was to be the first and last Victorian expedition effort.

THE CAMEL DRIVER Landells was giving the exhausted camels rum to help revive them! Burke flew into a rage about this practice so Landells quit. Burke then foolishly smashed up all of the rum bottles.

THE DOCTOR, Herman Beckler, was adamant that it was unsafe to continue inland in the hottest part of the year. He wisely quit at Menindee.

BURKE AND WILLS' SUPPLIES included 120 small mirrors, which they planned to give to the Aborigines as gifts.

AT COOPER CREEK Wills wrote that the Aborigines were "mean-spirited and contemptible in every aspect". Later, his opinion was to change when hospitable Aborigines gave them food and help. Had Burke not fired at one of them for trying to steal an oilcloth, all of the men might have survived.

DURING THE JOURNEY sickness and starvation made Charles Gray so weak he had to be tied onto his camel.

THE SEEDS OF NARDOO were ground up into a flour and made into cakes. They contained a lot of starch and fibre, but very little vitamins or minerals.

ABORIGINES ALSO GAVE THEM the leaves of the Pituri plant, which Wills observed, *"has a highly intoxicating effect, even when chewed in small quantities"*.

Surprisingly, one of Australia's least successful explorations, has become one of the most famous. A string of fatal errors turned a well-equipped Victorian expedition party into a fiasco and led to the doom of all but one of the men.

ROBERT O'HARA BURKE, a police inspector and sergeant, was an unlikely man to lead an expedition into some of Australia's most inhospitable country. Added to his lack of experience were his impatience, bad temper and a reluctance at first to travel lightly (and therefore more quickly). Burke's second-in-command soon quit and his chosen co-adventurer became the young surveyor William Wills, an amiable and weak man who may not have perished with his impulsive leader had he stood his ground. As it stands, their names are now inextricably linked with the expedition's catalogue of errors.

DESPITE THE EXPEDITION LEADER'S SHORTCOMINGS, the party was very well equipped — £12,000 was put up to fund the mission and no expense was spared. When the men left Melbourne on 20 August 1860 they took with them 18 men, 28 horses, 24 camels (which they had imported from India) and an astonishing 21 tonnes of supplies. These included tents, a library of books on exploration, camp beds and 454 L of lime juice and rum. By the time they reached Balranald, Burke was becoming impatient to move faster. He was aware that John McDouall Stuart was also on expedition, and he despaired of being beaten to the punch. On the way, Burke dismissed some of the party and dumped sugar, tents and the life-saving lime juice. At Menindee, more men extricated themselves from the expedition, including the camel master and doctor. On 19 October, a reduced party of eight men and one Indian camel master pushed on to today's Queensland border.

Above: The smell of the camels rankled the horses and the bullocks, so the animals had to be kept apart, forcing the party to advance in two lines.

GLORY AND CONSEQUENCE

On 20 November, on the banks of Cooper Creek, Burke made a decision that was to have disastrous consequences.

With summer fast approaching, the sensible thing would have been to wait near the string of waterholes, making small excursions and retreating to Menindee if necessary. Burke, keen for glory, decided otherwise. Leaving three men under the command of William Brahe to set up a depot (Fort Wills) at Cooper Creek, he travelled on with Wills, Charles Gray, John King, six camels and Burke's horse. Brahe maintained Burke told him to leave the depot if the party took longer than three months to return. The men were 1100 km from the Gulf with the aim of trekking the path beaten by Sturt in 1845. They had three months, the hottest of the Australian calendar, to make an epic journey.

WITH THE EXCEPTION of dry, sandy ridges fringing Sturt's Stony Desert, fresh water, grass and food were plentiful on the journey to the Gulf, which they reached on 11 February 1861, although not to the sea. The trip had taken two months and two-thirds of their stores — the return journey would claim much more. Heavy storms bogged down the camels, the humidity was stifling and Burke fell ill after eating a snake. Gray was found stealing flour, so Burke gave him "a good thrashing" in the words of Wills. With supplies low, they ate the first of their camels in March 1861. On 10 April, Burke's horse, Billy, met the same fate. Six days later, Gray became the first human fatality.

KING, WILLS AND BURKE struggled on, arriving at Cooper Creek on 21 April. By unhappy coincidence, Brahe had left that morning. All they found was the famous Dig Tree and, buried nearby, 23 kg of flour, 27 kg of oatmeal, 27 kg of sugar, 7 kg of dried meat and 10 kg of rice. The men were not to know that Brahe was camped only about 14 km away! Burke's decision was not to follow the party, but head for a police outpost at Mount Hopeless, some 240 km south-west. They buried a note explaining their intention, but forgot to burn another note on the tree telling rescuers to dig.

REINVIGORATED, the men set off. Within a fortnight, the last two camels died and the billabongs ran dry. Aborigines gave them fish, rats and Nardoo while the men awaited rain or rescue. Brahe, meanwhile, had travelled back to meet the main party, who were killing time at Menindee. He found the camp in a shambles and the men riddled with dystentery and scurvy. Along with William Wright, Brahe decided to return to Cooper Creek in the event Burke and Wills had returned. The Dig Tree seemed undisturbed, so they failed to notice the men's return.

BURKE, WILLS AND KING were less than 48 km away, subsisting on rats and Nardoo. Wills returned to the tree on 30 May 1861, but found nothing new. By 22 June, Wills, who felt "completely reduced", was unable to walk. Their only help lay with the Aborigines. Burke and King set off to find them, but Burke collapsed and died on 30 June. King returned to Wills to find he had also perished. Months later, King was found living with Aborigines.

Left: Burke, King and Wills trek back to Cooper Creek in this painting by Nicholas Chevalier.

Left to right: William Wills (1834–61); setting out on the mammoth trek in 1860.

the FACTS!

DESPITE THE consequences of the journey, Burke and his men travelled approximately 2250 km and succeeded in crossing the continent from south to north.

A FAMOUS OPERA SINGER of the time named Julia Matthews gave Burke and Wills each one of her white leather gloves. Burke was in love with her, but his love was unrequited. He took his glove on his journey with him and it was lost; Wills left his at home and it was later sold at auction for $2300.

THE SIGN carved into the Dig Tree at Cooper Creek (below) read: DIG 3 FT NW. APR 21 1861. Sadly, this living piece of Australian history was vandalised and burnt down in 2002.

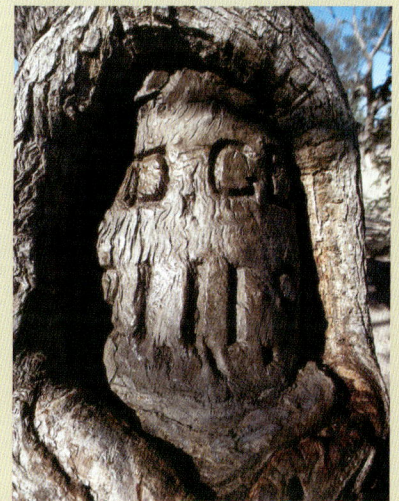

"THEY APPEARED TO FEEL great compassion for me," King wrote about the Aborigines who took him in for two months.

WHEN HIS RESCUERS came across the scrawny, semi-naked, badly sunburned King, one said, "Who in the name of wonder are you?" "I am King, sir ... the last man of the exploring expedition," the emaciated man answered.

Above: John McKinlay (1819–72).

the FACTS!

JOHN McKINLAY set out from South Australia on the same day that Landsborough left Moreton Bay for the Gulf on board the *Firefly*.

THE MESSAGE LEFT UNDER the Dig Tree was finally found on 28 September 1861 and the unlucky truths of the expedition revealed.

THE ABORIGINES WHO HELPED King were given gifts by Howitt and his party. Among the presents was 23 kg of flour, which the Aborigines called "white fella Nardoo".

IN A FINAL CRUEL STREAK of bad luck, the carrier pigeons that Howitt released to send news of discovery of the bodies of Burke and Wills were pounced upon by kites and killed.

McKINLAY'S PARTY was lucky to survive their mission. Soon after they had eaten their last camel, they chanced upon the salvation of a station outpost on the Bowen River.

LANDSBOROUGH also discovered the Barkly Tableland and the Georgina River, which he called the Herbert River.

WALKER HAD BEEN A commandant of Native Police but was sacked for being inebriated.

The search
for survivors

The disappearance of Burke and Wills' party prompted a slew of expeditions to search for the vanished explorers. Rescue parties from Victoria, Queensland and South Australia were quickly dispatched.

Of course, all of the rescue parties were too late to help Burke and Wills, but they did discover John King and learned the place and manner of Burke and Wills' demise. Many of the search parties also found excellent grazing land in Central Queensland.

THE MOST successful search party was Alfred Howitt's, which set out in June 1861, a few days before Burke died. Howitt first interviewed Brahe before travelling to Menindee and on to Cooper Creek, where he too failed to dig and find Burke and Wills' message. Party member Edwin Welch came across the scrawny, sunburned King, who told his account of the disaster and led them to Wills' grave, which also contained his journals. Burke's body was also recovered. Dingoes had ravaged both of the unfortunate men's remains.

Above: Burke's decomposing body was wrapped in a Union Jack and buried beneath a box tree, but was later returned to Melbourne for a State funeral.

BEFORE HOWITT RETURNED with news of the bodies, a second party was sent to the Gulf and joined by a Queensland contingent led by 36-year-old Scotsman William Landsborough, who discovered pastoral land around Richmond, Hughenden and Cunnamulla. South Australia had also sent John McKinlay north from Gawler in late September 1861. McKinlay found Charles Gray's grave and followed the Albert and Leichhardt Rivers north to the Gulf by 20 May 1861 — a distance of over 3200 km. The last rescue party, with Frederick Walker in charge, set off in September 1861, but heard Howitt's news in 1862 and quit.

Left: William Landsborough (1825–86). His reports of Gulf country farmland enticed settlers to the Queensland outback.

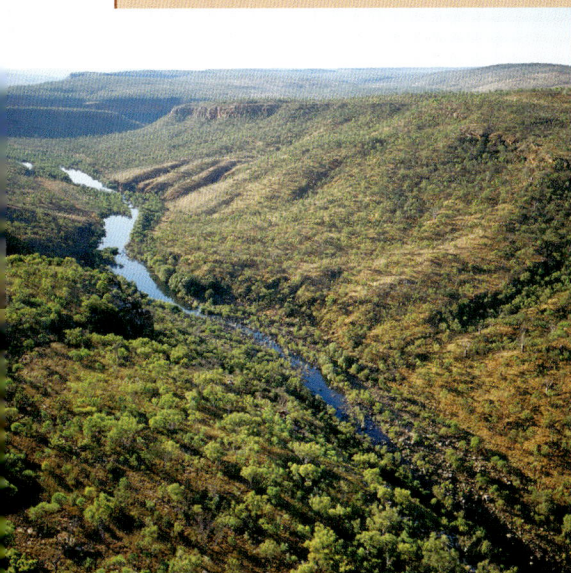
Above: Forrest's 1874 expedition party.

Western frontiers
— the Forrest brothers

The Overland Telegraph Line, which largely followed Stuart's route, opened up central Australia and made accessible the already discovered lands to the east. The west and the arid inland remained the last frontiers of Australian discovery.

ABORIGINES made claims that there were fine lands and the bones of white men in country north-west of Perth. John Forrest was appointed to ascertain the truth of these reports in 1869. He found no traces of the human remains or excellent farmlands described, but he did get a taste for exploration that would see him lead another expedition in 1870.

THE AIM WAS to travel inland from the Great Australian Bight, going in a different direction and on a more extensive route than Eyre's travels 30 years beforehand. The party departed from Esperance on 9 May 1870 and were to meet the ship

The ship *Adur* was able to anchor in only two safe harbours, as much of the coast along the Bight is rugged and steep.

Adur at the harbours of Eucla and Israelite Bay. Still no inland lakes or rivers were found. On 17 July 1870 they reached the head of the Bight and arrived in Adelaide on 25 August. Forrest had discovered grasslands from Eucla to Fowlers Bay, but no water to maintain them. However, the expedition paved the way for a telegraph line to be built to Western Australia in 1877. His third expedition in 1874 covered country between Perth and the centre, and met up with the Overland Telegraph Line in South Australia. The expedition found pastoral land and springs that later comprised part of the Canning Stock Route.

FORREST'S YOUNGER BROTHER Alexander joined him on his 1874 expedition. Alexander is best known for his later forays into the Kimberley region in the late 1870s, when he discovered Fitzroy Crossing and the Oscar and King Leopold Ranges, as well as the Ord River and the lucrative goldfields of Halls Creek.

WHEN THE PARTY WAS coming to the end of their water and rations, Alexander Forrest and Tommy Windich pushed on to reach Peake Telegraph Station at the end of September 1874. There they were able to receive help for the other expedition members.

Left: The King Leopold Ranges were a natural barrier. "I have never exerted myself so much in my life," wrote Forrest.

the FACTS!

JOHN FORREST'S PARTY also stopped to celebrate Queen Victoria's birthday, this time with a 21-gun salute.

ALEXANDER FORREST wanted to trace the Ord River to its sea outlet in Cambridge Gulf, but limited rations would not allow the detour.

THE RICH GRAZING LANDS Alexander Forrest discovered were quickly snapped up by settlers on inexpensive long leases or bought outright for just ten shillings (the equivalent of $1) an acre.

ANOTHER FORREST BROTHER, Matthew, accompanied Alexander on his Kimberley exploration.

THE LAND John Forrest found was not very impressive. He noted that the grassy areas were "so isolated ... that it would never pay to stock them".

JOHN FORREST (below) was elected Premier of Western Australia in 1890.

Above: Ernest Giles (1835–97).

Through the centre
— Gosse, Warburton & Giles

Forrest's west–east journey was matched by two expeditions in the reverse direction. Major Peter Egerton-Warbuton and William Christie Gosse both quickly arranged voyages through the centre, but it was Ernest Giles who made the most extensive travels through the inland.

the FACTS!

WHILE STARVING in the Gibson Desert, Giles came across an abandoned joey. He "*pounced upon it and ate it, living, raw, dying — fur, skin, bones, skull and all*". He also remarked, "*The delicious taste of that animal I shall never forget*".

TO AVOID THE HEAT, Warburton travelled a lot at night, navigating by the stars.

WARBURTON CAME close to death several times. On 12 November 1873, when supplies of flour, tea and sugar were completely exhausted, he wrote, "*Unless it please God to save us, we cannot live more than twenty-four hours ...*" The men were saved when Richard Warburton shot a small bird, which they devoured hungrily.

> **PETER EGERTON-WARBURTON**
> LEFT THE KNOWN HERE FOR THE UNKNOWN
> ON APRIL 18TH, 1873
> WITH HIS SON RICHARD, J. W. LEWIS, DENNIS
> WHITE, CHARLEY, SAHLEH AND HALLEEM.
> AFTER SUFFERING MANY PRIVATIONS, HUNGER
> AND THIRST CROSSING THE GREAT SANDY
> DESERT THE PARTY REACHED ROEBOURNE W.A.
> WITH NO LOSS OF LIFE ON JAN. 26TH. 1874
>
> ERECTED BY HIS RELATIVES
> TO COMMEMORATE THE 100TH. ANNIVERSARY OF
> HIS DEATH NOVEMBER 5TH. 1889.

GOSSE WAS A SENSIBLE and considerate expedition leader. He abandoned the race towards Perth when his party began to suffer, writing, "*The safety of my party obliges me to give up all hope of advancing further*".

GILES DISCOVERED Lake Amadeus, where his horses quickly became bogged up to their knees in the thick, salty mud. Luckily, they eventually struggled free.

AT ALMOST 60 years of age, Warburton was considered too old to receive government support on an expedition, so the South Australian Government chose Gosse as the man to trek through unexplored lands in central Western and South Australia. Undeterred, Warburton enlisted the help of his friend Thomas Elder to fund his own expedition. He took with him his son Richard, five other men and camels as pack animals.

Above: Malleefowl meat nourished Ernest Giles.

GOSSE, MEANWHILE, left Alice Springs with a party of eight just eight days after Warburton's expedition had departed. He covered far less territory than Warburton but became the first European man to lay eyes on Uluṟu, on 18 July 1873. Warburton's expedition party was ravaged by sickness and hunger, but managed to travel approximately 6500 km to complete the first crossing of the inland from the centre to the west.

Above: Lake Amadeus with Kata Tjuta beyond.

ERNEST GILES was an accomplished bushman. From 1873 to 1876 he made many expeditions through some of the toughest terrain in the world. Giles named the Gibson Desert after a member of his expedition, eighteen-year old station hand Alfred Gibson. Gibson and Giles were travelling west from the Rawlinson Ranges when they ran desperately low on food and water. Gibson decided to go back to the main group for help, but became lost on the way and was never seen again. Giles, travelling only a few kilometres a day and suffering intense thirst and hunger, eventually made it back to camp and named the desert after his friend.

Below: Gosse first described Uluṟu, which he named Ayers Rock, only as "a high hill". On getting closer, he was astonished by the "immense rock, rising abruptly from the plain".

The sights
they saw

Australia's diverse landscapes, from desert to subtropical rainforests, formed an ongoing panorama of strange beauty. The plants, animals and landmarks the explorers recorded often astonished those who stumbled upon them.

LAKES, RIVERS, DESERTS, MOUNTAINS — all manner of landscapes, most as unlike the English countryside as possible, were laid before the telescopes of explorers. Some sights evoked dismay and others were overlooked, with the explorers either failing to recognise the mineral wealth before them or seeing the vistas in the wrong season, thus missing the beauty of desert wildflowers or the sight of the mighty River Murray in full flood. Many travellers were surprised to find that previously explored country differed greatly from earlier accounts. The most celebrated finds were waterways and grazing lands. Later, mineral wealth brought a flood of treasure hunters from around the globe.

GEOLOGICAL FEATURES AND LANDMARKS were not the only remarkable sights that the explorers relayed. Naturalists, such as Ludwig Leichhardt, made keen observations of the nature around them and collected botanical specimens. They cleared up the incorrect assumptions of earlier navigators, actually finding and recording animal species only glimpsed years earlier from the shore.

Above: Giles named Mount Olga (now Kata Tjuta) on 14 September 1873 and remarked on the "rounded minarets, giant cupolas and monstrous domes" of these "vast and solid, huge, and rounded blocks of bare red conglomerate stones".

LATER, WILLIAM HORN and Charles Winnecke's findings on the Horn Scientific Expedition in 1894, would further zoological and botanical knowledge of the continent. On this journey, a team of university professors and scientists, ranging from geologists to ornithologists, travelled by camel from Oodnadatta to Mt Stirling and east to Alice Springs, making many important observations and discovering the Water-holding Frog and the Painted Dragon, among other species. The Royal Geographical Society encouraged such expeditions, but ceased providing funding after the failure of Albert Calvert's scientific exploration in 1895, during which two men died.

Left: Burke and Wills saw two Brolgas on the Burke River — their furthest inland record of this species.

the FACTS!

EVEN IN LATER YEARS, when the bulk of the continent had been explored, small pockets hid surprising secrets. Carl Lumholtz was to find and describe Lumholtz's Tree-kangaroo (above) in a small pocket of rainforest in north Queensland in 1883. He wrote, *"It is not necessary to describe my joy at having this animal, hitherto a stranger to science, at my feet".*

GEORGE GREY, exploring near the Glenelg River (WA) in 1838 was shocked to find Aboriginal artwork of a robed, hooded white figure.

STURT DESCRIBED IN DETAIL the habits of the Stick-nest Rat and collected a specimen of the Spinifex Pigeon (below), noting that the little pigeon appeared to like "basking in the tremendous heat".

THE HORN Scientific Expedition of 1894 charted over 7 million ha and added over 170 species of spiders, reptiles, beetles and molluscs to Australia's biological lists.

JOHN LORT STOKES described flying-foxes as a "huge flock of screeching vampyres".

Above: Norwegian Carl Lumholtz (1851–1922) recorded nature and Aboriginal customs of north Queensland.

the FACTS!

LUDWIG BECKER, Thomas Baines, William Westall, Robert Elwes, Augustus Earle and other artists captured the stark simplicity of landscapes and the weary existence in explorers' makeshift depots.

FERDINAND VON MUELLER (below) was a prolific collector of botanic specimens. He was the Victorian Government botanist from 1853, and was later director of the Royal Botanic Gardens, Melbourne.

THOMAS BAINES, the artist on Augustus Gregory's expedition, was a brave and dependable man. Gregory even entrusted him to sail the boat *Tom Tough* to Timor to restock supplies. He completed this 1200 km journey successfully.

ERNEST FAVENC explored from Queensland to Darwin in 1878 and later wrote a book about exploration.

EMILY CAROLINE CREAGHE accompanied her husband Harry on Ernest Favenc's expedition. She kept a record of the trip from a woman's perspective and entitled it *The Little Explorer's Diary*.

A record
on the road

Few of the fascinating details of Australia's exploration would be known were it not for the records kept by naturalists, artists, botanists and the explorers themselves. Diaries, journals, illustrations and photographs have provided lasting records of incredible lives.

MANY OF THE ADVENTURES undertaken, when examined in retrospect, appear courageous but extravagant, daring but often foolhardy. However, that so many journals survive is testimony to the careful consideration of these men. Few of them were unaware of the danger they faced. Even fewer of the diaries record regret, even in the face of death, but almost all of them express a gamut of emotions from hope to despair, delight, fear and salvation. Some, such as Giles' journal, were superbly written; others, such as those of Burke and Wills were little more than scrawled notes with gaps where it may be presumed their time was filled simply with the struggle to exist.

Left: Ludwig Becker's watercolour of the camp he shared with Dr Beckler at Menindee on Burke and Wills' fatal expedition.

THE END OF AN ERA

By the dawn of the 20th century, the early exploration of Australia was largely exhausted. Gone were the days of men on long-suffering beasts making that last daring dash across the continent for glory. It now lay with squatters, drovers and settlers to take up the baton of discovery. In fact, in 1895, the South Australian president of the Royal Geographical Society wrote:

The chapter of Australian exploration closed as it began, with deeds of splendid endurance and courage, with deeds of awful suffering, and with the loss of heroic lives. I say 'closed' for it can not be supposed that any other expedition will ever be fitted out, for there is nothing more to discover.

HE WAS WRONG on that count. Many more adventurers would succumb to the desire of discovery. Even in the last decade, finds such as the ancient, presumed extinct, Wollemi Pine remind us just how little we still know about the land around us. New or separate species of animal are still being classified. Fascinating archaeological finds are being made. Centuries-old shipwrecks are coming to light. Perhaps one day DNA technology will reveal the final resting place of pioneers such as Leichhardt. In any case, a trip to one of Australia's spectacular historic or wilderness areas still promises to reveal small yet personal discoveries.

Bibliography

Allen, J. L. Dasch, E. J. & Gough, B. M. (Eds). *Explorers from Ancient Times to the Space Age Vol 1*, Simon & Schuster Macmillan, Princeton, USA, 1999

Baker, S. *The Ship: Retracing Cook's Endeavour Voyage*, BBC Worldwide, London, UK, 2002

Barwick, J. & J. *Explorers of Australia: Coasts and Mountains, Australian Exploration from 1770 to 1830*, Echidna Books, 2000

Barwick, J. & J. *Explorers of Australia: The Deserts and Beyond, Australian Exploration after 1840*, Echidna Books, 2000

Basset, J. (Ed). *Great Explorations: An Australian Anthology*, Oxford University Press, Melbourne, Australia, 1996

Basset, J. (Ed). *Great Southern Landings: An Anthology of Antipodean Travel*, Oxford University Press, Melbourne, Australia, 1995

Brasch, N. *The Early Ocean Explorers*, Reed International Books, Port Melbourne, Australia, 2005

Cannon, M. *The Exploration of Australia*, Reader's Digest, Sydney, Australia, 1987

Clark, M. *A Short History of Australia*, Penguin Books, Sydney, Australia, 1992

Favenc, E. *The History of Australian Exploration: 1788–1888*, Golden Press Pty Ltd, Sydney, Australia, 1983

Feeken, E. H. & Gerda, E. E. *The Discovery and Exploration of Australia*, Thomas Nelson & Son, Melbourne, 1970

Fern, A. & Llewellyn, D. *Australia's Best Heroes & Adventurers*, Harcourt Education, Reed International Books, Melbourne, Australia, 2004

Flannery, T. *The Explorers,* The Text Publishing Company, Melbourne, Australia, 1998

Fox, A. *Wild Habitats: A Natural History of Australian Ecosystems*, ABC Books, Sydney, 2007

Gard, S. *A History of Australia Vol 2: Early Contacts*, Macmillan Education, Melbourne, Australia, 2000

Gard, S. *A History of Australia: The Colony of New South Wales*, Macmillan Education, Sydney, Australia, 2000

Giles, E. *Australia Twice Traversed from 1872–1876*, DoubleDay, Sydney, 1889

Jeffreys, M. *Murder, Mayhem, Fire & Storm*, New Holland Publishers, Sydney, Australia, 1999

Jones, C. & Parish, S. *Field Guide to Australian Mammals*, Steve Parish Publishing, Brisbane, Australia, 2005

Laidlaw, R. *The Land They Found: Australian History for Secondary Schools, Third Edition*, Macmillan, Melbourne, Australia, 1979

Poignant, R. *Discovery Under the Southern Cross*, Collins, London, UK, 1976

Robinson, J. *Captain Cook's World*, Random House, Sydney, Australia, 2000

Ross, S. *Conquerors & Explorers*, Alladin Books, London, UK, 1996

Russell, J. *Australia's Explorers*, Heinemann Library, Reed International Books, Melbourne, Australia, 2000

Salentiny, F. *Encyclopedia of World Explorers: From Armstrong to Shackleton*, Dumont Monte, London, UK, 2002

Slater, P. *Amazing Facts about Australia's Heritage*, Steve Parish Publishing, Brisbane, Australia, 1992

Tiley, R. *Australian Navigators*, Kangaroo Press, Sydney, Australia, 2002

WEBSITES

www.gutenberg.net.au/explorers.html
www.australiassouthwest.com
www.rahs.org.au
www.librariesaustralia.nla.gov.au
www.captcook-ne.co.uk
www.abc.net.au/navigators
www.win.tue.nl/~engels/discovery/pacific.html
www.maritimemuseum.com.au
www.freeread.com.au/ebooks/titles-aus.html
www.adb.online.anu.edu.au/adbonline.htm

IMPORTANT DATES

1606 — Willem Jansz makes first landing on mainland. Louis Vaez de Torres discovers Torres Strait.

1642–43 — Abel Tasman discovers Tasmania and New Zealand.

1699 — William Dampier writes the first European account of the kangaroo.

1770 — James Cook claims eastern Australia for Britain.

1788 — Governor Arthur Phillip and the First Fleet arrive in Botany Bay to establish a settlement.

1792–93 — Bruny d'Entrecasteaux charts southern Tasmania.

1798–89 — George Bass and Matthew Flinders circumnavigate Tasmania.

1800–02 — France sends Nicolas Baudin to map Tasmania.

1802–03 — Flinders circumnavigates Australia.

1804 — Settlement established by David Collins at Hobart, Tasmania.

1813 — Blaxland, Wentworth and Lawson cross the Blue Mountains.

1818 — Louis Claude de Freycinet is sent from France to follow up Nicolas Baudin's work.

1823 — John Oxley discovers the Brisbane River.

1824 — Hume and Hovell cross Australia from east to south and sight the Alps.

1826–27 — Penal colony established at Moreton Bay, Qld.

1829 — James Stirling established settlement near the Swan River, WA.

1834 — Lhotsky is first to explore the Alps.

1835 — John Batman finds and settles the site for Melbourne.

1836 — George Kingston discovers the Torrens River and Adelaide is proclaimed.

1840 — Count Strzelecki becomes the first European to climb Mt Kosciuszko.

1844–45 — Leichhardt crosses the continent from Brisbane to Port Essington.

1860–61 — Burke and Wills travel from Melbourne to the Gulf, but perish on the voyage.

1862 — John MacDouall Stuart forges the path for the Overland Telegraph Line.

Index